Literacy
Through
the
Book
Arts

Flight the Kite
BY Robert

Flight the Kite
BY Wesley

Flight the
Kite by Joanne

Flight the Kite
BY stephen potter

Katie The Kite
by Leanne Evlin Mary Lou

Flight the Kite
by Shane

Literacy Through the Book Arts

PAUL JOHNSON

HODDER & STOUGHTON
London Sydney Auckland

Hodder and Stoughton Ltd
Mill Road
Dunton Green
Sevenoaks
Kent

First published in 1993 by
Heinemann
A Division of Reed Publishing (USA) Inc.
361 Hanover Street
Portsmouth, NH 03801
USA

Books in the Nursery (page 85) first appeared in *Early Education*, No. 3 (Spring 1991), and was reprinted in *Nursery World*, Vol. 91 (July 1991).

Parts of "The Psychology of the Fold" (pages 26–41) were originally published in *English in Education*, Vol. 25 (Spring 1991).

A CIP record for this title is available from the British Library.

ISBN 0 340 59540 X

To dear Ercelia for so much

"And what is the use of a book," thought Alice, "without pictures or conversations?"
Alice's Adventures in Wonderland
Lewis Carroll

contents

acknowledgments

I am indebted to the following schools for giving general permission to reproduce the work of their pupils:

Beaver Road Infant School, Manchester
Beaver Road Junior School, Manchester
Christ the King R.C. Primary School, Manchester
Lower Park C.P. School, Poynton, Cheshire
Mills Hill Primary School, Oldham
Moorside Junior School, Trafford
Norbury Hall Primary School, Stockport
Rose Hill Primary School, Stockport
St. Thomas CofE School, Oldham
Urmston Infant School, Trafford

Every attempt was made to receive permissions from the parents of children whose work is reproduced here but this was not entirely successful. The author apologizes to parents who he failed to contact in this way.

Also to the following headteachers and teachers who have given me so much personal help and encouragement: Beryl Edwards, Ercelia James, Rosemary Jeffries, Marlene Lawrence, Patricia Locke, Margaret Symons.

Many thanks to my students of the Manchester Metropolitan University Art and Literature course, who have provided me with so many wonderful book art visual aids from which to select illustrations.

Finally I want to express my indebtedness to Judith and Mac who have, as with all my texts, used their expertise in English to reveal all my grammatical shortcomings and inconsistencies.

introduction

Book Beginnings...

It is a cliché to say that we live in a world of visually communicated messages, but it is true. Every street, shop, magazine, even junk mail that comes uninvited daily, conveys information that is 75 percent visually oriented. The linguistic material is carried by visual means too: the shapes and color of letter forms are art. The TV media is visual, and computer language is increasingly visual in character. So why is it that the curriculum, which is where children acquire the skills to shape their lives, patently disregards visual communication generally, and, more specifically, ignores the part it plays in literacy?

There are many reasons for this, which I discuss later, but my thesis is that the concept of book art elevates both words and images to a heightened level of communication. Even the phrase "book art" is problematic. It is the word "art" that causes all the problems. We are conditioned to think that the very stuff of books—words—are somehow a visual abstraction; that the design, illustration, and presentation of books have nothing to do with *Words*; that these things form a kind of appendage tacked on to the linguistic symbology just to enable it to "become."

After all, don't we just "write" a book and get the publisher and a team of designers to do the rest?

There is a growing school of literacy educators on both sides of the Atlantic who are questioning this monolithic view of writing, and I refer to them here; but I hope that the work of children in the book art genre presented in these pages will speak louder and with greater pragmatic authority than the experts can. Coexisting words and images—the interdependency of the two great communication systems of literacy and visual communication—is the most powerful force of intellectual and emotional development we have. And the book form is the most potent way of housing that force.

This is a very personal book, written about myself as a paper artist and my journey from that starting point into children's self-made books. My life in and out of education interacts constantly. The English educator, Fred Sedgwick, is right when he says "He who only education know does not know education." Consequently, this is not a report or analytical study into children's literacy through the book arts but a largely autobiographical account of children I have

1

taught—or, more especially, *am* teaching—and what I think their books tell us about their ability to communicate, and how the book concept enables that communication.

I came to words because I came to love paper, and from paper to books, and from books to everything that the book takes into itself and transforms wonderfully. There is so much that needs to be experienced about the spirit of paper. The book artist is handicapped without sensitivity to it, for this sensitivity makes the book into an object of sculpture. And once you see the book as sculpture or mini-architecture, it can do things for you that you would not think possible. Some of our most gifted children's picture book creators have discovered that fact, and many of the children represented here have discovered it too.

Much earlier, in my sketchbooks and journals, I had found that when you join words and pictures a heightened meaning is possible. But when I came to make a book myself, everything seemed to switch into a new gear. I could explore not only two symbolic systems simultaneously but also the surface that gave those systems life. It was a revelation to me, and I have not yet come down to earth from that initial encounter.

And so in my teaching I found that the book, being part of me, slipped into my relationships with children. It seemed to work the same mysterious power for them as for me. The book was its own inspiration. Words demanded to be written in one. Writing became an excuse for making a book, not making a book an excuse for writing.

Constructing books, in a binding sense, can be an engaging experience, and there is most certainly a place for it in schools. I have taken another path, and one more inspired by the East than the West, in order to arrive at book concepts of extraordinary simplicity yet remarkable versatility when brought into contact with the instinctive creativity we all possess.

The books reproduced here are frozen episodes in a child's evolving experience of communicating. So where relevant, the progression of individual children's development is shown, and the processes of setting out and arriving discussed. All the illustrations attempt to reveal something about children—their cognitive development in the main—that the book art activity has provoked. Whatever proposals others may wish to make formulating a book art methodology, it is always the intuitive responses of children to the book arts that give the sharpest clarity to the concept. We have forgotten how to use our intuition in teaching; fortunately, children have not been purged of it yet, and so it is we who have to change. Making books may be a problem for us, but it is not for our children!

All the work has been drawn from three sources. First, my own week-by-week commitment to one school in particular has yielded a rich supply of book art projects. Second, I have "commissioned" groups of children in schools scattered about Greater Manchester to make books. The groups are of mixed age and ability, and my intention is to work with them right through their schooling. I visit these schools on average once a month, discuss with the groups the books they are making, and suggest new, ongoing developments. They, in turn, return to their classrooms and share their work with their peers. Third, by developing a relationship with individual teachers who, through their own personal vision, have fostered book art programs with their children, I have found a continual source of book art.

What I find stimulating and moving is the indefinable way that each child brings something of his or her own to the book form. It is an all-embracing concept, reaching out to every part of human experience and drawing a spontaneous response from children—not just a piece of writing or drawing but the making of an object loaded with personal meaning to be cherished and valued. Nothing stimulates children more than the sense of achievement that the book art object symbolizes. And there is no better stimulus for making a book than the one that has gone before it. Consequently, book art is most effective in the classroom when it is developmental. There is ample evidence in this book to prove that. The book art concept is not yet another new subject to be squeezed into the curriculum: it is the most effective way of processing the whole curriculum!

I have not gone out of my way to show examples of good practice, but, rather, an across-the-board range of work. In some cases the work is a result of a programmed approach; in others, children have simply been given a blank book form and left to get on with it. While this is not a technique I employ myself, I must say that some books produced in this way have been a revelation to me.

The fact of the matter is that a book can be anything you want it to be, and that is part of its mystery. What I say to myself when confronted with a child's self-made book is, What has this child learned about the book concept? And how has the book concept been changed by this child's work?

All real learning is experiential. If you are not already into making books with children, then use this book as a means of achieving that end. I promise that you won't find that process disappointing.

part one

chapter 1

The Book Puzzle

Why is it that while most learning comes through books,
so little is processed through the book form?

It is Susan on the phone. She is three weeks into my Monday evening children's book art course. "What do you think?" she says excitedly. "John, who hates writing and will do anything to avoid it, made a book two days ago. He hasn't stopped writing since!"

I am delighted for both Susan and John. I am also pleased that John is not an isolated case, for one of my many pleasures of running the Book Art Project throughout schools in the U.K. is that reports of successes like John come to me daily. But what is the nature of this remarkable phenomenon, which grasps children and holds them to its bosom?

What are the book arts? This question is often put to me. Rather like asking for a definition of a piece of music or a poem, it is not an easy one to answer. In fact you are likely to get as many different answers as people prepared to answer it. Does it mean the art of making a book or making art books? What components make up the book arts, and are they the prerogative of the expressive arts or can they embrace the humanities and sciences too?

Much has been written about those peculiarities that collectively form the book—typography, cover design, suitability of paper, binding methods, wood-block illustrations, calligraphy, to name a few. But what is the relationship between what these elements serve—the book as *content*—and what they are—the book as art *object*? Writers and makers of books so often perceive their roles as independent of one another, and this has something to do with the book dilemma and its curious nonparticipatory place in education. Just how vulnerable is the book?

All the predictions of the 1960s that the book genre would be obsolete within the decade, replaced by microfilm and electronic retrieval systems, have proven ill-founded. The book, in and out of world recessions, is healthier today than it has ever been. To the bibliophile it is not just a container of words and graphics; the book has an inbuilt psychology of its own. There is a vast body of research into the suitability of typefaces, page design, size and format, binding methods, and presentation ethos. The magazine *Visible Language* is one of the main disseminating organs of analytical research into the visual forms of language, including the book concept, historically, psychologically, socially, aesthetically, and emotionally. (Some articles have addressed the effect of the aroma of book paper on the reader. Is the tactile "feel" of some papers more suitable for projecting poetry than others?) Yet the book is something of a mystery, not easily explained by taking it to pieces and analyzing the parts. It is so many things to so many people in so many different circumstances. In the course of two hours we may experience a magazine, a railway timetable, a novel, a street map, a business report, our diary, a menu—all book forms to a greater or lesser degree. Printed words, illustrations, diagrams, maps, photographs, and charts—forming a collective symbology we call the book form—bounce in and out of our social and professional lives with such rapidity that we hardly notice them. But somehow that flat, sandwich-like package is a mystery; it is the most public and private of all objects, for we communicate to the world through it and commit our deepest and most intimate feelings to its protection. It has the power to change people beyond measure, and some have even laid down their lives for it.

It was that mystery that first drew me to it and which holds me there still. It started for me when, as a child, I accompanied my father on his sketching trips in and around the medieval city of Norwich, where I was born and spent my childhood and youth. I don't think I can ever remember my father when he wasn't wearing a large, floppy raincoat. In the seemingly huge pockets that hung from it like kangaroo pouches he carried his sketchbook and a collection of pencils, all held together by a thick rubber band. His tiny pocket money allowance was spent almost entirely on books, mainly about art and music, his two passions in life. So it was that I came to perceive books in two ways: those you took things out of with your eyes (published books) and those you put things into through your eyes (sketchbooks). Later, when I went to art school, that dual aspect of the book was given official approval. We had to keep a sketchbook in which we

would make annotated drawings and use the art books in the library to familiarize ourselves with the work of "The Greats." When I subsequently trained to teach, my sketchbook became more of a notebook for a while, as it swung from a personal to a didactic use. Around this time, the mid-sixties, it was becoming fashionable to replace the sketchbook with a camera. Students at elite London art colleges burnt their sketchbooks as a symbolic act of defiance. The camera, it was held, had made the sketchbook redundant. Fortunately, I was too old to be engulfed by this iconoclastic movement that found its voice in pop art, and I fear a whole generation was denied the enrichment of a sketchbook because of it.

Visiting art college degree shows today I see that the sketchbook is far from dead, and indeed more alive than we would have thought possible in the sixties. Pages are cut and rearranged, objects glued and stitched in, mixed media abounds—paint, pencil, crayon, collage, photographs, even plaster of Paris; some books are so solid with additions that they remain permanently open at 180 degrees! For these students the book form is a versatile continuum for holding and assimilating ideas that will not only influence the art and design they produce but the lives they lead. I notice too that words play almost as large a part as the visual material in these books. Perhaps art schools are more likely to promote learning through these two modes of communication than any other educational institution. Do students of other subjects have something to gain from this approach to communication?

Today, drawing is again encountering the intense scrutiny it received in the 1960s. For some, electronics has replaced drawing on paper and sketchbooks have been replaced by computer printouts. But only a few children will eventually find their way into art school or teacher education, and for them the developmental sketchbook/notebook will not exist. Does this matter? Will anything be

Page from Sue Hunter's visual journal 1990–1991.

missing from their lives? What I don't think ever occurred to us as students was to relate the art book we read and looked at to the *art book*—for that is what a sketchbook is—we were making. Yet are the two concepts that different? We were unconscious of the fact that the book we were "making" was already made, that the fastened paper of regular size, texture, and quality dictated, to a greater extent than we were aware, the marks we put in it.

In the twenty-five years that have intervened since I was in art school, drawings, graphic diagrams, musical scores, visual poetry, and paper environments have preoccupied my creative life. But it wasn't until the mid-eighties that I began to think again about what had

held those ideas together for me for so long—the mystery of the book.

It is so *practical* to make a book of words, graphics, and pictures, whether the aim is to explore one's creative potential (an illustrated poem) or make a scientific investigation (inventing a machine). Even in this electronic age the notebook has a valuable function; the jotting down of words or graphics is as essential to the programming of a thought as it was to Leonardo da Vinci. And "practical" is the operative word. The pen or pencil symbolizes through direct line work on paper. There is no system to be processed—as in computer technology—before ideas can be expressed; the computer's own language has to be understood for it to be of any use. But the book has other uses than its facility to hold direct, spontaneous explorations. Some book forms can be opened out flat, like a mural, so that everything one has prepared, or is preparing, can be seen at a glance. Comparisons of and reference to several pieces of work can be visualized and synthesized simultaneously. The computer, invariably operating on one screen, cannot offer so immediate a service, even with printout visualizations.

But the book is where we discover most about ourselves. The journal, diary, notebook, sketchbook are all systems that make meaning possible. Some people write; others draw; some do both. The diaries and letters of the literati reveal some of the most perceptive observations of their time. The sketchbooks of Turner and Picasso are illuminating in showing the visual journey they made in arriving at their seminal work. The notebook sketchbook is a great liberator of the imagination because it falls outside the hierarchy of "Art." One is permitted to produce lesser-art in them, to be adventurous and capricious, and in doing so the freedom to be oneself can produce visionary statements that would otherwise not be made in the more conscious pursuit of excellence. But most importantly, it is the psychology of making a book that is so compelling. The organization and development of ideas through the discipline of paginated sequence of writing and/or visual statements has produced some of the greatest achievements of civilization. Yet all it is, is a bundle of papers joined together.

Making a crafted book oneself as a home-based pursuit began to be popular in the nineteenth century. The justification for home bookbinding lay not so much in providing the binder with a way of preserving his or her own writings as in providing practicable means of rebinding published books. Bookbinding as a "useful craft" was encouraged so as "to afford to book owners sufficient elementary information to enable them to bind books so that they will become handy, manageable and durable appliances of the home, and always available for instruction or recreation" (Crane, c. 1900). The task was an exacting one, and even if the home bookbinder didn't have the necessary skill or equipment to make a near perfect model of the genre, he could "take his cases to some neighbouring professional bookbinder and get him to letter them in gold." It wasn't long before the useful craft of bookbinding found its way into the school curriculum, and by the 1930s it was firmly established alongside woodworking and weaving. It had its spiritual genesis in William Morris (1880): "What else can we do to help educate ourselves and others in the path of art, to be on the road to attaining art made by the people and for the people as a joy to the maker and the user?" Morris promoted the medieval illuminated book as the quintessence of book concept and design, the inspiration of which led him to found the legendary Kelmscott Press in 1891. Unlike Morris, school bookbinding was less concerned with realizing beauty through functional design as with "recognised utility." The aims were to work systematically and accurately; to exercise patience, economy, and order; to appreciate good design and workmanship; to be ready to be critical; and to equip children "to express themselves in joyous combinations of form and colour" (Collins, 1936). This last part, taken from a school bookcraft manual, is the only reference to what might be termed "creativity," and nowhere is there a suggestion of how the pupils might personalize the contents of the book they make.

By the post-war period the notion that children were creative and expressive as a consequence of being human was gathering momentum, and this revelation focused attention on the blank paper that was accommodated by the craft of binding. The usefulness of craft bookbinding could now include in its terms of reference the concept of the book as a repository for the binder's own expressions. School bookbinding manuals after the war provided both for traditional conservation practice and for the growing trend in encouraging creativity. This latter development is also evident in the attention given to binding. Whereas the inside of the crafted book had hardly changed at all structurally during the millennium, the cover had always been the place where the bookmaker could let his hair down. In the Middle Ages this extended to decorating the cover with solid gold and precious stones, so that it often resembled a richly adorned wedding cake. By the late twentieth century creative bookbinding had gone into a stratosphere of its own, producing astonishing adventures into sculpture and mini-architecture. In some cases the book—as words on pages—appeared rather insignificant against the extravaganza of glass, metal, and flashing lights that encapsulated it. In the more restrained climate of the classroom these flights of fancy were reduced to children designing book cover patterns made from vegetable prints, block prints, combed painting, and stipling. There was something very homespun about this, and one can see once more the influence of Morris and the Arts and Crafts movement. Robin Tanner, the visionary educator and etcher, played an important part in revitalizing bookcraft in schools in the post-war era. However, Seonaid M. Robertson felt compelled to agonize in 1952: "Why is junior bookcraft so depressingly

Crafted books, 19th–20th Century. Collection, the author.

dull? I believe it is quite simply because it is taught as though it were an exercise in arithmetic, as though there were one correct product to be turned out at the end of the lesson identical with every pupil."

One of the best books to emerge from this surge of interest in the book crafts was Pauline Johnson's *Creative Bookbinding* (1963) based on her children's bookbinding courses at the University of Washington. She not only included Eastern bookbinding methods (which most bookbinding manuals fail to do), but placed child-orientated bookcraft within an historical and cultural context. About half the book is taken up with cover design, which indicates the progress that the homemade book had made by the 1960s. But even as late as 1978, Leslie Bennett and Jack Simmons, in a rare and sound primer on basic bookbinding with children, barely comment on the notion that the crafted book should somehow be related to its contents. Almost as a postscript they suggest that the book's pages are like a container in which something can be poured. "Books can be *filled* with written work of all descriptions and covering all areas of study" (my italics). How children conceive, construct, or plan this written work on these pages is not discussed. In fact, during this whole period, and one might be tempted to say up to the present time, the crafted book in education has been poised on the brink of having its contents used for something. But no writers seem at all certain what that something is or how it should be structured to become an integral part of the book.

This concept of a finished book of blank pages, leaving aside the notebook/sketchbook, diary, or similar usage, is unprecedented in the whole history of the book genre. It is our compulsive need to communicate that necessitated the invention of the book. The development of the printed book, from the fifteenth century to the mountains of books on every conceivable topic published in just one week today, is due to the single fact that humankind has so much to say about everything.

So how is it that the foundation of bookmaking in schools is about the communication of absolutely nothing? How could so many children through so many decades make so many books of blank paper resembling Dadaist manifestos? And ultimately: How is it that over a thousand years of processing and disseminating knowledge through the book form should have so little impact on the way children learn to develop?

I don't think I've ever met anyone who doesn't, in their romantic daydreams, want to write a book. It is commonplace to say that we all have a book inside us. Even my great-aunt Alice, who did little else than attend to her husband and two lodgers all her life, was fond of saying, "One day I'm going to write it all down in a book." Celebrities who have been hoodwinked into believing they have no writing ability employ ghostwriters to write the fact and fiction of their lives. Many beginners turn to the kiss-of-death "vanity" publishing firms in desperation to see their words in print.

Children are inundated with books from the beginning of school, and often earlier. Most schools I visit are well stocked with story and reference books, although sadly many of them are out-of-date. Story books represent the groundwork of children's reading and writing. Reference books provide a gateway to knowledge. If, then, the source of so much enlightenment comes from the book form, is it not reasonable to suppose that children's learning should be processed through the book concept too? What are the alternatives? It is no accident that the book concept has stood the test of time. There is little that can be achieved on single sheets of unbound paper. The standard exercise book, the bastion of children's graphic communication, is problematic because one is unconsciously conditioned by its structural intransigence. I remember at school having "project" exercise books that had alternating lined and unlined pages. The nuisance was that you always wanted a drawing page when there was a lined one, and vice versa. The ready-made writing book not only dictates the nature of the content but the form as well. Its internal psychology restricts the communicating vision of the creator because, in a sense, it is already finished and complete—nothing else need be added to it.

Teaching colleagues not infrequently comment on the frightening prospect that a whole exercise book, comprising as many as fifty pages, has on children. Inwardly they are saying, "How can I fill all these pages?" To be faced with an empty book of pristine paper may be a challenge to a professional writer, but to a child it can be a prison.

Now *writing* a book is not necessarily synonymous with *producing* a book, as many budding authors soon discover. Presenting a publisher with a *fait accompli*—a word-processed and bound book—can often lead to disappointment when the writer discovers that while it works in its present form, it certainly is not suitable for publication. Knowledge of how books are made, from concept to design to printing and binding, is essential to a writer, saving hundreds of wasted hours creating a book that is impractical or uneconomical in publishing terms. The convention of structuring a book in permutations of thirty-two pages establishes a discipline which conditions the author's method. There is a challenge in programming thought in this way, and this can lead to insights and improvements to the material as a whole, as one must condense or restructure one's thought to match the book's structure. Approachable classics like Ruari McLean's *Typography* (1980) illustrate the sophistication of the design of books, a harmony between the author's intention and the designer's insight.

Taken from this perspective, the reason why children are so rarely encouraged to structure thought in the book form would seem to be because the task seems so dauntingly complex. The compromise solution is for children to either make books in the tradition of pre-war elementary school bookbinding or to make very basic books. The problem with the craft bookbinding approach is that the style of presentation, like the exercise book, is prescriptive. Or at least that is what tends to happen. Children provide the needs of bookbinding, not the other way around. With the basic book approach, folded sheets of paper are stapled together or loose pages held together by string tied through punched holes. These are satisfactory as far as they go, but where they usually fall down is in their appearance. Pages of unrelated size and proportion are bundled together and stapled. Inconsistency of style and presentation reduce the all-important visual impact of the contents.

The National Writing Projects of both the U.S. and the U.K. have promoted parent and child writing collaborations. It is not unusual for books to be made in this way and for illustrations to be incorporated into the activity. All this, of course, is excellent, but it is so easy for the book art element to lean towards a supportive, even peripheral, role, a kind of bag to put the writing in, and not a multicommunicational concept of which writing is only one of the crucial components.

For Oscar Wilde style was everything, and those whose profession is producing books seem to agree with him. It is not just that one's sense receptors intuitively demand that which is visually satisfying, but that the *manner* in which thought is manifested conditions the *process* of thought.

When children plan and design a book of their own, integrate handwriting, lettering, illustration, layout, and binding as a vehicle for the communication of ideas, a superior kind of mental activity comes into play. It is enlightening to watch children involved in the task of making a book, from concept to completion, for the sense of personal satisfaction is infinitely greater than if shortcuts are used to arrive at a finished book. This does not mean, however, that children's book art is necessarily a time-consuming process. A substantial part of my book art dissemination program is occupied with showing teachers how simple origami books can be, comprising, for example, front and back covers and three integral double pages and made in just a few seconds from one single sheet of paper. Indeed, the simpler the mode, the wider the potential for creativity it offers.

By preparing margins and borders, both vertically and horizontally, children learn to structure their writing in finite areas: to look ahead and gauge whether or not the next word can be fitted into the space provided or, alternatively, placed on the next line. Even more significant is the demand of the page, fitting into it an appropriate part of the story or study that matches an illustration on the facing page. When children are presented with a small-format page to contain all that can be said about a character in a story or the rose bay willow herb, the mind is concentrated wonderfully. What is to be put in and what is to be left out? What could be a more useful learning skill than the ability to condense an idea and express its essence?

So why is it that the book form has been so consistently bypassed in the curriculum as a tool for processing thought and feeling? To find an answer one must first look at the history of the book. In the Middle Ages the holistic ethos of transcendentality united everything aesthetic. The book shared common status with all that was made to celebrate the glory of God. Thus cathedrals and all they contained—stained glass, mural painting, altar pieces, vestments, furniture, and liturgical books—had equal status in the corporate symbolism of glorification. The great illuminated manuscripts of the twelfth century—The Winchester Bible, for example—rank amongst the greatest works of art produced in Europe at that time. Christopher de Hamel (1986) says that these were almost certainly painted by the scribes while they were writing out the books. Looking at them one does not sense that the visual material—

A range of origami book styles.

pictures, decorative borders, ornamental headings—are inferior to the text. Indeed, the penmanship is visually played down, monotonous in its regimentation, for the scribes were well aware that color and form can reveal through visual reality what words cannot do themselves. While it would be a false analogy to compare medieval artists with writers, illustrators, designers, and binders of later times, this intrinsic harmony between the visual and literal aspects of the book changed radically with the Renaissance. The invention of movable type was one factor; the other was the application of scientific method to the forms of expressive communication, the compartmentalism of the arts. The effect of this was that writing and painting became two distinct operations, which were brought together only when the nature of the book's subject required it. The concept of the book as an integration of linguistic and visual symbols died. The Renaissance established a cultural hierarchy in which the concept of a "work of art"—painting or literature—had high status. Objects that had a utilitarian function or were a hybrid of more than one aesthetic domain had a low status. It is obvious into which of these two categories the book would find itself. It suffered on two accounts. One was that it could be *used*—indeed that was its function—and so it was not a pure "art" form; and secondly, it was a fusion of two discrete systems—words and art. This historical anachronism is as firmly in place today as it was five hundred years ago. Present-day painters exhibiting in major art galleries and the prizewinning literati are afforded high status with incomes to match, while the books that have brought them to the public's attention and assured their success are low status. Books are conveyors, vessels rather than originators of art per se.

If one translates this into the school curriculum one can begin to see the dilemma of the book concept in education. The book,

having no real aesthetic status of its own, hovers in a no-man's-land betwixt English and art. Both areas acknowledge it, use it extensively as a teaching aid, but refuse to identify with it. Thus children write stories and collections of poems, produce critical studies and historical, geographical, or scientific projects that, to all intents and purposes, are books in concept without them being recognized as such. Similarly, bookbinding, illustration, lettering, and calligraphy are visual design areas acceptable to "art" curricula but only as definable craft-design skills. The way in which they compose the essential components of the book concept, and indeed are meaningless without it, is ignored. The literary meaning of the crafted words of lettering or the story-oriented context of illustration is treated as if it is not really there at all. In fact it is the very link with linguistic concepts that has been responsible for placing these skills towards the bottom of the visual art hierarchical structure.

And this is why for over sixty years children of the Western world have been producing crafted books of vacant paper. In one conceptual sense the pages have to be there to make the book what it is, but in another conceptual sense the pages don't exist. This paradox accounts largely for children not making books in a holistic way.

But there is another reason for the absence of the integrated book form in schools and why, while books flourish in society generally, they are not made by children as vehicles of learning. I can best describe this with an anecdote. Two or three years ago a friend, a talented and successful writer and illustrator, was eager to work with children on a writing and illustrating project. The local schools were more than keen on the idea. I contacted the area art adviser for assistance and support. After weeks of getting nowhere and much prevarication I confronted him with the proposal in person. "I would like to be able to help," he said, "but I really can't use my budget for supporting a writer. Try the English adviser." The eventual reply from that quarter was, "Sorry, but I can't support an illustrator from the English resources."

Neither English, art, nor, for that matter, any other subject in the school curriculum system will take responsibility for housing the book arts. In the world outside education, artists, writers, musicians, actors, and dancers seem to work amicably together. Free from the constraints of educational ideology, the decision to collaborate is a mutual and politically uncomplicated one. Some of the most exciting aesthetic innovations this century have been cross-arts collaborations: to name two—in Europe, Cocteau, Picasso, Stravinsky; and in the United States, Cage, Cunningham, Rauschenberg. In the book art context there are many examples of close relationships established between writers/poets and illustrators—Roald Dahl and Quentin Blake spring to mind—and sometimes, as in the case of Maurice Sendak, they are one and the same person. But in education the delineated expressive areas tend to preclude interrelationships of any real substance, even historically sound ones like the book form. Ken Robinson (1990), Professor of Arts Education at the University of Warwick and chairman of the National Foundation for Arts Education, articulates the problem when he says:

> The overwhelming majority of what actually goes on in the arts outside schools and the committee rooms of education seems to be combined. What is an opera in these terms? Is it music or drama? What is film—visual art or theatre? What is performance art? Music theatre? Kinetic art? Oral poetry? Storytelling? Carnival? If the critics of combined arts tried to impose their will on the arts outside schools,

much of contemporary artistic life would have to stop.

Teachers of younger children are perhaps more able to accommodate the book arts in the curriculum because the subject structure is less overt in the elementary/primary school than in the high/secondary school. But here the problem is one of a different kind. Ironically, it is the closely guarded sophisticated art and literary skills of specialist teachers that keep the book arts from older children; and the very lack of those skills among the generalist teachers that produces the same result with younger children. The package of writing, illustration, design, et al. appears, on the face of it, far too demanding for teacher and taught. A teacher in a recent course said to me that she wanted to make books with her children but "couldn't justify the time it would take with all the other curriculum subjects to teach." I tried to convince her that the book arts is just a way, in my view the best way, of processing most—if not all—of the curricular subjects. Writing, illustrating, design, diagramming *is* the very substance of processing knowledge. Book art *is* the curriculum, not just an adjunct to it.

For the sake of our children we need to find a way back to the wholeness of the individually made medieval Book of Hours, to integrate it with the diversity of the post-Renaissance printed book, and enrich that with all the book-transforming innovations of the post-war period to the present day. If we start with the concept of the book as a human-made device for celebrating all that is possible, and even more than possible, and let that guide our teaching strategies, classroom practice, and curriculum structures, the dynamism of the genre itself will do the rest. Through that experience children enter into, and become part of, their cultural heritage, for the book is their birthright.

chapter 2

The Two Literacies

Linguistic language and visual language have coexisted on the page since the beginning of the book. But do they combine to create meaning? And if so are there implications for children's own book art?

It is normal to think of literacy as the prerogative of reading and writing. But in recent times the term "visual literacy" has been much used by art educators. Kurt Rowland, the influential writer on visual communication in education in the sixties and seventies, saw pictorial composition as comparable to written composition: that a successful arrangement of shapes in a drawing was metaphorically analogous to a collection of words and punctuations strung together to make a well-constructed expressive sentence. It is popular to talk of the *grammar of art*. Just as successful writing involves a whole range of connected elements—structure, grammar, syntax, spelling, punctuation, economy, cohesion, continuity, style, wit, imagination— so successful artwork requires the same analogous components. Also, by using terms like literacy and grammar there is, one might be forgiven in thinking, a political attempt to make art more acceptable in the curriculum, to cast it as a serious subject like writing and not the laissez-faire subject it is often perceived to be.

It could be said that the concept of art as a language, as essential to communication as linguistics, had its roots in the Bauhaus. Of all the brilliant artists/teachers amassed there in the twenties and thirties, Paul Klee was one of the most articulate in discussing the meaning of marks on paper. For him, every line had an intellectual and emotional meaning. He performed a Freudian-like psychoanalysis on art and discussed how concepts of time, space, movement, imagery, structure, relationships can be systematically expressed through line and color. His teachings have permeated modern art education, but has the concept of art as a superior communication system really been taken that seriously in the curriculum?

A great deal has been written about children's literacy development, from research into the sociology of reading to children at home to "let's-make-writing-fun" type books. Equally, art educators have produced a welter of books, from studies into the psychology of children's drawing to manuals on art techniques. What has been markedly missing in both literacy and visual camps are publications that discuss the relationship between the two. I already have stated the causes of this void. The demarcations of the Renaissance and the structural politics of the curriculum make for definitive territories of learning and educational shortsightedness. The training of specialist teachers invariably precludes interaction. Language experts feel inadequate in discussing children's visual imagery, which is matched by the literacy inexperience of art education experts. Ironically, what is for many children a very intuitive action—linking writing and drawing—is not at all intuitive for most educators!

Lucy Calkins (1986) has been instrumental in showing that successful teaching of writing grows naturally out of the teacher's own writing and creativity. But with what frequency is the writing experience of teachers related to whatever visual experience they may have? In her book on authors as visual artists, Kathleen G. Hjerter (1986) says:

> The subtleties of form and color, the distinctions of texture, the balances of volume, the principles of perspective and composition—all these are good for a future writer to experience, and will help him to visualize his scenes, even to construct his personalities and to shape the invisible contentions and branching of plot.

Her list includes e.e. cummings, William Faulkner, Goethe, Victor Hugo, Rudyard Kipling, Edward Lear, Robert Louis Stevenson, Evelyn Waugh, and Rabindranath Tagore.

But do the languages of art and writing identifiably interact to make a dynamic, intercommunicating force? In the analytical studies of illustrated books there is noticeable caution in lifting the veil between the two. John Lewis (1967), in focussing on the illustration and design of books in the twentieth century, examines movements like German Expressionism and the wood-engraving

revival in England and France. Many books on the genre linger on what is arguably the greatest period of all, the Middle Ages, and in these the social, historical, political, religious, and aesthetic ambience dominates the text. Some concentrate on the monastic establishments in which books were created and others on the calligraphy of the period. Several comprehensive studies have been published about illustration in general and children's picture books in particular. In one study, Barbara Bader (1976) says that illustration hinges on the interdependence of pictures with words, on the simultaneous display of two facing pages, and on the drama of turning the page. In its own terms its possibilities are limitless.

> A child's understanding outstrips his vocabulary. He recognizes things before he can name them, but until he can name them he doesn't really know them. . . . hence his satisfaction in pictures of the commonplace. . . . they confirm his existence.

Referring to the writer and illustrator Tomi Ungerer, Bader extols the "extreme mobility of his illustrations. He moves through the book like a film director. . . . a new fluidity. . . of picture book movement." Similarly, Marcia Muir (1982) comments on the inherent meaning in children's book illustration:

> The artists' imagination should be fired by some aspect of a story so that there is a fusion of ideas and an extension of meaning. . . . Artists of reputation may create picture books, but however beautiful they may be and however they may be praised by adults, the final criterion must be that the book involves the child emotionally and intellectually.

John Ryder (1960) gets near to describing the power of art to transform a story to a higher level of consciousness when he says,

Illustration can add something to a story that is not in the story itself—the authentic typographical or architectural background, for instance, or characteristics of dress and manners. A painterly-draughtsman-illustrator will be competent to describe, in visual terms, the psychological nuances leading to, or arising from, an incident. In this way, rather than through tiny little drawings depicting "hair raising episodes" will the child gain something from the illustrator.

Douglas Martin (1989), in his essays on fifteen contemporary book illustrators, celebrates these same virtues of draughts-manship and the irreducible vision of the illustrator to tell "another" story in addition to the written one. He quotes Charles Keeping, comparing the relationship between word and illustration with that of jazz musicians playing together. The notion of a dialogue between words and images is now under much discussion, and indeed the trend in picture books today is towards a polyphonic inter-mingling of the two. Referring to the husband and wife partnership of Janet (illustrator) and Allan (writer) Ahlberg, Martin says,

Figure 2–1. In these pages from *Beth* by Sarah (8) additional information to the text is contained in the artwork: in one, the places on the island, and in the other, the potion ingredients. In both cases the information is communicated more by drawing than words.

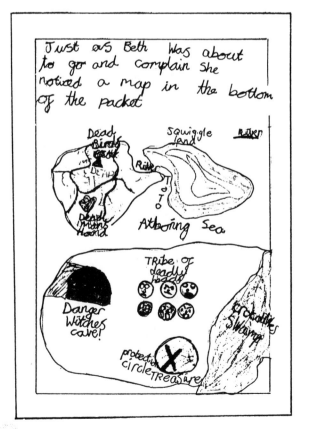
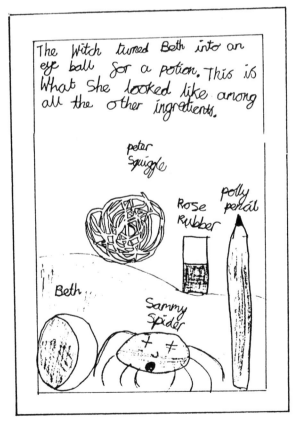

By the early 1980s the Ahlbergs had found many ways of associating words and images which resulted from using numerous spot or marginal drawings in contrast to a sequence of full-page spreads. These little drawings are ingeniously threaded through or clustered around a concisely tailored text, with the result that the "mind's eye" is made to work hard without knowing it. The words in any case are calculated to trigger independent visual images. The reader's eye flits to Janet's tiny vignettes and back, having collected the requisite information. Sentences and jokes begin in words and end in pictures. A question or blending of two or three words can lead into a pictorial list that can be named or described at will, or into alternative visual scenes which may be visited in any order to spark off further observation and storytelling.

Now these studies echo the belief that illustration is a communication strategy par excellence, at once part of, and yet independent from, the text. Moreover, picture books of the eighties and nineties seem to be moving into a new homogenization phase, in which both symbologies weave in and out of each other effortlessly in graphic manifestation on the book page. Never before have we been made more aware of the image on the picture book page. Yet the authors of these studies inevitably lean in a visual, rather than literary, direction, so an analysis of how words and images penetrate one another is underplayed.

Conversely the same is true. John Rowe Townsend's (1990) continuously revised compendium of books written for children on both sides of the Atlantic refers to children's book illustrations and picture books (making quite rightly a clear distinction between the two), but his insightful comments are based essentially on literary merits. Indeed, books about children's literature tend to concentrate almost exclusively on the text, and some writers behave as if illustrations are not there at all. "The relation of pictures to stories and the nature of the reader's interaction with both are an important aspect of literacy too little

regarded and even less understood," says Margaret Meek (1991). But is it surprising, considering the training of academics and teachers? If we have a degree in English, it is unlikely that our training included any form of visual study. If we studies art as our main subject at college, chances are that the written word did not come our way that often. Meek's view is that children's illustrated stories owe as much to the film and advertising media as the history of literature. We live in a world dominated by visual images, and telling a story in words and pictures is a way of recording the world.

> Picture books . . . make reading for all a distinctive kind of imaginative looking. Without the pictures, the text is decontextualized, and without the text, the pictures are only part of the full texture, the counterpart of the artist's meaning.

Children should be encouraged to linger and explore what they see because readers, artists, and writers create the world of literate seeing.

The awareness of the influence of what children read on what and how they write has made the context, structure, and content of children's books come under scrutiny. This has led to a reevaluation of picture book art, as a gleaning of magazines like *Children's Literature in Education* (international) and *Signal* (U.K.) will evidence. David Lewis (1990) argues that picture books of all kinds are inescapably plural. They always require a command of two different forms of signification. He calls this the verbal, or textural, and the pictorial, or ironic.

This evolving concern for the status of children's book illustration runs parallel to, and is part of, the trend towards children learning through looking at pictures. Bay Hallowell Judson (1989) notes the increasingly popularity of the notion that people need help in learning to look at pictures. The case for the need to learn how to read, or decode, visual images is currently being made in

Tomorrow shall we go to Africa, and you can be the captain?

From *Granpa* by John Burningham. London: Jonathan Cape 1984. (Reproduced by arrangement with Random Century Group, London.)

many quarters. One result has been to bring artists and their work to the attention of children, producing much that is exciting and innovative in our schools. Writers' and artists' school-based residencies have helped to remove the mystique that so often surrounds them.

What is needed is a new kind of educator who embraces the two prime communications systems—writing and visual communication—in a pragmatic and down-to-earth way. One such person is Judith Graham (1990). She discusses the ways in which picture books depend upon, teach, and reward active participation in their readers. She rightly dismisses those who see illustrations as a distraction, robbing the child of the personal meaning his or her own visual associations draw from the story. We live in a visual world of images in which we find meaning. Those images are part of our visual apparatus, and when children look at book illustrations they bring to that experience a great deal of stored visual information. Graham divides the visual

semantics of picture book illustration into four categories—people, settings, story, themes—and, through carefully selected reproductions, shows how just a slight turn of the head or the suggestion of night by the crescent moon can add a new dimension to a story. The art materials that illustrators use feed the emotional richness of the visual experience. For example, Charles Keeping's individualistic illustrations were sometimes made on layers of perspex (Plexiglass), which gave them a depth unlike any other illustrator's work. Graham's discussions with children using one of his books leads her to say that examining the strangeness of his strong and resonant images with them enabled them to absorb some of the power and beauty of the story it accompanied. Towards the end of her book, Judith Graham talks in what I can best describe as loving detail of John Burningham's picture book *Granpa* (1984). When Granpa dies, the deep and incomprehensible loss to the little girl who has been his close companion is symbolized by his empty chair at one extreme of the double spread and the little girl at the other. The empty, wordless space between the two is loaded with a vast devastating silence. This vacuum filled with visual meaning transcends words. We need more books like Graham's, which penetrate deep into the language of illustration and reveal its potential in child development in the same way that children's literature has been disseminated.

Perry Nodelman (1988) covers similar ground in his study of the narrative art of children's picture books, including the contextual meaning of visual objects and an examination of time and action in illustration. This is a much welcome analysis of the psychology of visual perception in picture books.

Just what is it that art can do that words cannot? Is there a domain of understanding that only linguistics can elucidate? The illusion of three-dimensional space on the picture plane can express subtle psychological relationships between people and things. The symbolism of color and spatial depth is irreducible; it cannot be substituted with words. So is the atmosphere that an illustrator can produce by just a few lines and suggestion of texture. It is into this visual scenario that words come into their own, for while art is strong on describing the appearance of things and weak on expressing changes through time, words are strong on describing actions. In painting, a figure appears in a desolate twilight landscape. Heavy pigment creates an atmosphere that only paint could communicate, but what the person is thinking can only effectively be conveyed by words. Art cannot say "tomorrow" or "in three years time I will be. . . ." And a whole spectrum of emotional feelings like "Am I really doing the right thing?" have more developmental possibilities through a verbal discourse than a visual one. Put simplistically, words are good at describing feelings and communicating time (words can't

accurately define the color of an object), and art is good at analyzing the appearance of things (observational drawing) but weak at communicating time. When the two are combined, as in picture books and the strip cartoon, each language supports and compensates for the limitations of the other. What a tragedy that for us adults, and indeed for children beyond a certain age, all the power of this fusion is underestimated in published books. When did you last see a novel with illustrations? It is not surprising that we can't see the potential of the picture book for children (or indeed the whole illustration genre) when it is denied in our own reading experience. We are visually illiterate, and that reduces their full meaning for us and, consequently, for the children we teach to read—but not "look" at—picture books.

All that has been said so far about writing and illustrating could be said of children's own creativity in the book genre. Over twenty years ago the psychologist Rudolf Arnheim (1969) was bemoaning the fact that words are given credit for nearly every cognitive function at the cost of that which is visually perceived and processed. When children are encouraged to illustrate their stories it is rarely applied with the same authoritative intensity and qualitative expectation as their writing. We tend to say, "If you finish your story in time you can illustrate it." And then do no more than distribute crayons and add a few weak words of encouragement. Yet the chances are they have by them on the classroom displays some of the great treasures of illustrated story books. Are we really so blind to the trans-forming power of visual imagery that we fail to see the potential of great books like Maurice Sendak's *Where the Wild Things Are* (1963), which "uses only 300 words to tell a story of Max and his visit to the land of the wild things, [while] his pictures tell a multiple of stories that *make more words unnecessary* (my italics) (Smith & Park, 1977)? Research into right-side brain behavior supports children's book art theory. Sinatra and Stahl-Gemake (1983) state that "visuo-spatial" ways of communicating and organizing meaning provide a firm basis for language work.

> A picture is worth a thousand words. The meaning of a picture can be comprehended in a single glance. . . . The visual imagery a person remembers due to pictorial input is recalled more rapidly, more holistically than the words the person uses to describe the images he or she is remembering. Research indicates that. . . a greater learning output was achieved when both brain hemispheres rather than one were activated in learning tasks.

The subject areas in which linguistic and visual modes coexist cover almost the entire curriculum. Mapmaking, automobile engine diagrams, and graphic notations are all visual techniques that define and communicate knowledge in geography, science, and music. Is there a curriculum subject that does not use graphic representation? What is needed is a new attitude to *all* forms of language/visual interaction in learning, to bury the naive and uninformed prejudice against visual thinking once and for all, and to elevate the book form as the superior *modus operandi*. Ruth Hubbard (1989) is one of the pioneers in this direction. Although her book is not oriented towards book art, she nevertheless explores the close relationship between children's writing and pictures and elucidates new insights into their creative behavior, largely drawn from her own experience.

The computer sciences have already taken the lead in reevaluating the two great communication strategies. Albertine Gaur (1984) argues that information technology has changed the way we not only think about writing today but the way we conceive the writing of the past.

Computers store information in an electronic memory by means of positive and negative impulses—the way information was once (during the age of oral tradition) stored in the human brain. With everything around us changing it is perhaps time to re-examine the concept of writing and look at it, not from the point of view of how effectively it can store language, but how effectively it can store information.

Computer technique is a multigraphic one. When visual images—diagrams, photographs, drawings—are so directly manipulatable and juxtaposable with text, the computer operator is, by virtue of computer language, a mega-image maker. A writer friend who used to send typed copy and separate graphic work to his publishers now does the whole word and image design process himself by desktop computer publishing. For the first time since the Middle Ages the writer, illustrator, and designer is one and the same person again. To be a writer isolated from other allied skills, like layout design, is no longer acceptable. One who processes ideas via the computer is *ipso facto* a mixed-media operator. And the computer phenomenon causes us to ask questions about our preconceived notions of writing outside the electronic media. A page of handwriting relates to, and is conditioned by, the page it is written on. Added meaning can be given to words by the way we write and draw them. Drawings and diagrams correlate with the words on the page. For children to develop, drawing, graphic, and design skills, as well as writing ones, are essential to their survival. One might say that their future depends on it.

What has gone wrong with literacy education is that the hierarchical exclusivity of the writing concept has made it insensitive to what happens around it on the page. Literacy has been overheating because we have been asking the question How does writing solve X? instead of How do the communication systems at our disposal solve X? Teachers of English at all levels of schooling must widen their vision and embrace what art and design has to offer them. It will change their thinking.

Now, children entering the dual-meaning environment of the picture book and extracting from it an enhanced understanding is not the same thing as children combining writing and illustration in their own work. There is an art/design/technology debate that is preoccupied with the question, Is creative drawing the foundation of design technology skills? The consensus view is in the affirmative. The skills developed in observational drawing are transferable to other forms of draughts-manship (e.g., architectural or engineering drawing) and computer graphics. If narrative writing is the foundation of other kinds of writing (e.g., reporting, describing, transacting, analyzing), the same can be said for illustration drawing. All that is gained from developing drawing skills in a story/illustration context has wide-reaching implications across the whole spectrum of functional design. Moreover, the closely allied writing/drawing skills of children's book art relates directly to the pragmatics of the communications media, advertising, and information technology.

Children should approach illustration not so much through illustration as through drawing. Illustrators Quentin Blake and Tony Ross draw in what appears to be a quick, improvised, almost sketchy style. Blake says that he arranges the composition of an illustration as the drawing progresses. If most people reading this, including myself, attempted to draw, say, an archbishop eating a sandwich while riding a tiger and added a background environment of rainforest or cathedral "as the drawing progresses," I think we would find that what might appear to be an unsophisticated skill is no such thing. To capture the essence of a facial expression or a specific figure or animal in movement comes from a special kind of imaginative intelligence.

Some seem to be born with it, but for most it is acquired through a systematic dedication to the drawing board. An illustrator's rapidly sketched figure is not the same thing as a child's matchstick man, for the artist's schema is retrieved from a bank of memorized images based on observation and resulting from perhaps years of experimenting in order to reduce imagery to the minimum of line work for the maximum of effect. On the other hand, the child's iconic imagery is incapable of transformation unless he or she is ready to enter into the ambience of developmental drawing. It is easy to be impressed with children's cartoon-type drawings, which are merely frozen effigies from a published source that has been memorized. Of course, some children have a bent for cartoon-orientated drawing and this is just as viable as any other kind, but one must be able to distinguish between creative and imitative habits of image making. Drawing is a language that can be taught to anyone, like writing, regardless of "artistic ability." Anyone who doesn't believe that should read Betty Edwards's (1979, 1987) books about drawing on the right side of the brain. The average child, like you and me, must arrive at illustration and book art design by using the same route as the professional; drawing from observation and imagination by building up a memory resource of images, analyzing, experimenting, inventing, exploring a range of media, and looking inquiringly at artists' work.

Children learn the art of writing by reading a wide range of material, and they learn how illustrations "work" by studying the artwork of picture books. But there are problems here. Allan Ahlberg has pointed out that while it can take only a few hours to write a picture book, it can take months or even a year to illustrate it. For a child to conceive "an old man lived in a bus on the edge of a field" is a different cognitive challenge than illustrating it. To communicate "old man" or "bus" through writing requires no more than the ability to write those words. But to *draw* them is quite another proposition. Children will say, "I can see it clearly in my mind," for the words trigger an internalization, but they soon discover that to draw that inward picture is no easy matter. All kinds of strategic questions arise. What does the bus look like? Is the man standing inside, outside, or on the steps of the bus? What are his facial features? Does he wear glasses? Is he old looking—if so, how do you make a drawing of a face that looks old? Apart from deciding where the narrative is to be placed on the page, stated words have none of these problems.

J. D. Stahl (1990) notes that just as literature for children was once closely linked to the acquisition of literacy, the development of a new form of interactive, participatory literacy is connected to the artistic ambitions of picture books and the art of "reading" them. He stresses that the picture book looks to the future and to a new form of pedagogy.

There is so much that needs to be researched into and reported about this "new form of pedagogy" and how these invaluable experiences can be acquired by children. How this might then relate to the processing of children's own book art is another story, one hardly started yet. The body of this book tries to show how some children, in some schools in the north west of England, have attempted to do this.

chapter 3

The Psychology of the Fold

Something quite wonderful happens when you fold a piece of paper in half—it becomes the first step in the journey to a book.

Although writing in some form or other has existed from early on in man's development, the first "books" were scrolls made in Egypt of papyrus around the fifth Dynasty (c. 2494–2345 B.C.). For over four thousand years the scroll held a dominant position in the countries of the Mediterranean world. There are examples of it rolled to one hundred and fifty feet on spindles turned by hand. (It must have been frustrating to have to roll back thirty feet of it to check on something that had been recorded!) The fold was not so much used because papyrus has poor resistance to manipulation. It was not until parchment was introduced that the fold came into its own and the scroll was rendered redundant.

The journey that the book then took—the codex form, comprising leaves bound one inside the other—is very much the story of modern civilization. However, in the East another, in some ways similar, development took place. According to Chinese records,

paper was invented in 105 A.D. and seems to have grown out of the knowledge of making silk. The hand scroll evolved from this, but it had the disadvantage of being inconvenient to store and awkward to unroll. The *kansubon*, or "rolled book," was the major book form for nearly a thousand years after its introduction into Japan in the fifth century. During the Heian Period (794–1185) several other book forms developed alongside the scroll. The basic one was the accordion book, constructed by folding the text of the scroll back and forth accordion fashion.

It is interesting how the cultures of East and West have taken such separate ways, not only in culture and religion but also (until recently at least) in the organization of systems of communication. Both experienced the birth of the book similarly—as a roll of vegetable fiber—but from then on, what happened to the psychology of the fold is completely different. In the West the fold was turned on the *inside* of the book, sheets placed one inside the other and bound down the center. In the East the fold was turned on the *outside* of the book, and the binding made along the side and not the center of the book. The history of both book cultures is a fascinating one, so different in every conceivable way. The great Biblical codices of the Middle Ages, ornamented with decorative texts and gold-leafed, brilliantly colored illustrations, is a style unknown in the East. Likewise, the school of Japanese polychrome wood-block printing, epitomized by the work of Hokusai and Hiroshige, are unparalleled in the West. Whereas the scroll did not survive significantly in Europe, its popularity in Japan has lasted to the present day.

Westerners' enthusiasm for the orient is part of their utopian longing, for the holist nature of the culture seems to be what is so missing from our own. In Japan the way one prepares to write, the way one writes, the instruments for writing, and the rice paper one writes on are united by a common philosophical and religious attitude to life. A great Japanese calligrapher once referred to calligraphy as a dance for the hand, and a sheet of paper as a great landscape. There is an organic wholeness about the appearance and feel of Japanese bound books that I find absent from those of our own culture, which somehow seem self-conscious in comparison. When I began my own book quest it was books of this kind that intrigued me most, and still do. It is the preoccupation with the magic of paper that has something to do with it (paper houses, kites, boxes, fans). The ancient paper-folding technique of origami has become something of a party-time cliche in the West, but it is sobering to reflect that its origins were functional, religious, and ceremonial. It was

Concertina book.

discovering a simple (one star) origami book, described in a book on origami, that led me to explore paper in my search for the book as a creative, living form. I was to discover that from this simple beginning over one hundred origami-like books were possible, some so complex that a degree in engineering would have aided their assembly!

Who, I wonder, was the first book artist to ask the question, How can I make a complete book from a single sheet of paper just by cutting and folding? A book must comprise folded units that are joined in someway. So taking a sheet of paper, the experimenting instinct is to fold it in half and then half again (see Diagram 3–1). Opened, this makes four units of regular proportion (Diagram 3–2). Folded down it creates a greeting card form, but hardly a book. Also, paper is usually supplied in rectangular proportions. The basic form can be of horizontal (landscape) or vertical (portrait) orientation (Diagram 3–3).

To make a book requires another fold. Open up the fold shown in Step 3 in Diagram 3–1 (Step 1) and fold on the vertical (Step 2). Open sheet (Step 3) and fold on the horizontal (Step 4). Fold into a concertina book (Step 5). Most books in both the East and West are conceived on the portrait rather than the

Diagram 3–1.

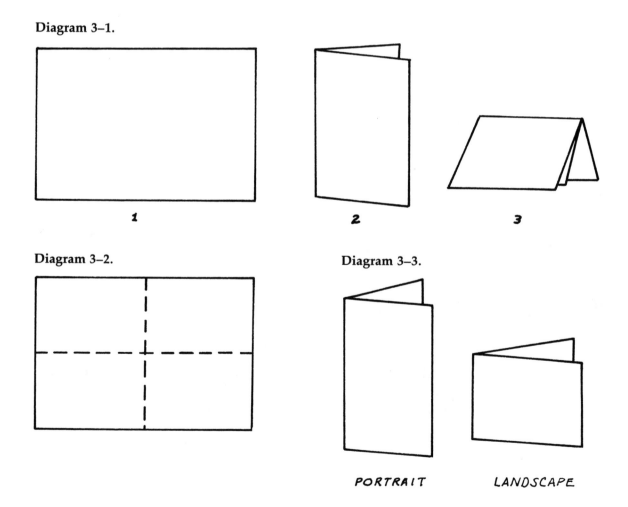

1   2   3

Diagram 3–2.

Diagram 3–3.

PORTRAIT   LANDSCAPE

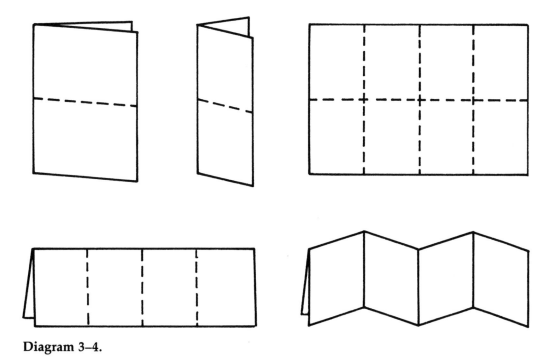

Diagram 3–4.

Diagram 3–5.

landscape orientation. Two explanations for
this are that shorter lines of writing are easier
to read than longer ones and that the vertical
book rests in the hands and on the book
shelves more comfortably. (An Oriental
explanation is that the vertical book symbolizes
vigor and the horizontal, passivity.)

Concertina (I prefer the word *concertina*
to the often used word *accordion*) and side-
bound books are almost unknown in the
West, at least where commercial publishing
is concerned, central binding being standard
practice. From a child's perspective the
Japanese-type book is easier to make. The
pagination of even a single-section European
book is a complex affair, the Eastern, a simple
sequence of paper. But where it serves children
best lies in the versatility of its presentation
forms: as a flat, panoramic form enabling the
whole book to be seen at once (Diagram 3–5),
as a tabletop three-dimensional form (Diagram
3–6), and as a book scanned in the conventional
hand-held way (Diagram 3–7). The concertina

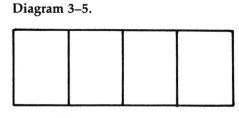

Diagram 3–6.

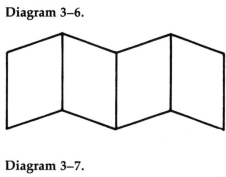

Diagram 3–7.

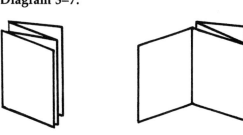

has also a vertical presentation (Diagram 3–8). Providing the concertina is "open bound," that is, the beginning and end are not held together by a commonplace spine, the book can be processed on both the front and back pages (Diagram 3–9). Another advantage is that any number of additional concertina units can be added simply by gluing one section to another (see Diagram 3–10). However a

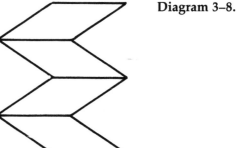

Diagram 3–8.

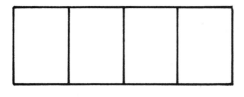

FRONT

BACK

Diagram 3–9.

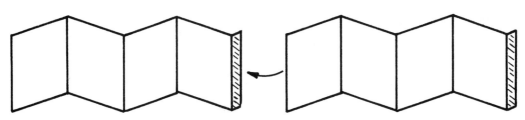

Diagram 3–10.

concertina book is made, leaving aside sophisticated binding techniques, it is always complete from the moment it is folded. In the style of presentation shown here, where the basic rectangular sheet of paper is folded on the horizontal before folding into a concertina, the double thickness gives extra strength to the book as a whole and the main areas of stress—the folds—in particular (see Diagram 3–11). In basic publishing terms the four-fold concertina has no competitor, for an eight-division format that can be folded flat can be photocopied and duplicated inexpensively before assembly into the folded book.

The simpler the structure of a thing the more you can do with it. But simple does not mean simplistic. As I have said, over a hundred different book forms can be constructed from one sheet of paper using the fundamental origami approach. The versatility of the concertina can be observed in its many uses as an expanding and contracting mechanism (see Diagram 3–12). Throughout the construction and interior design industries, the zig-zag form is widely used not only because of its strength but because it can freely stand of its own accord, hence screens, partitions, and fences.

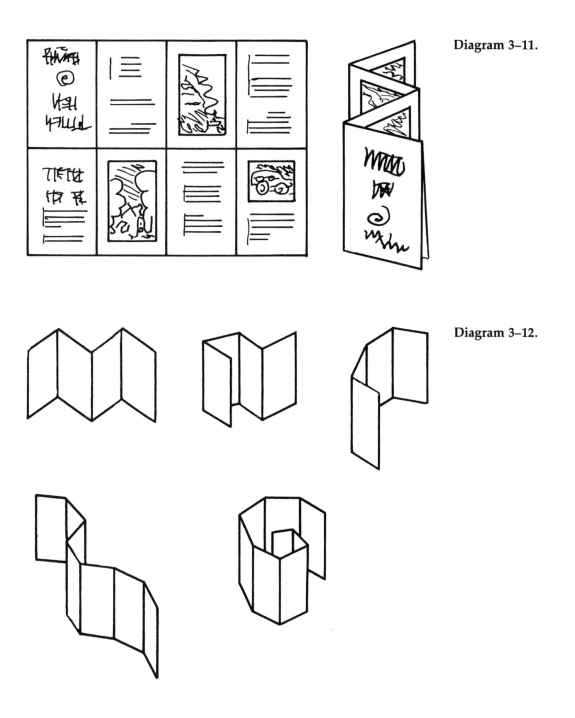

Diagram 3–11.

Diagram 3–12.

Advertising mail invariably comes in one form or another of the concertina fold.

In its primordial state the book is an object, a piece of paper architecture. When I was young, like many children I derived far more pleasure from building with playing cards than playing card games. It was a real challenge to see how high a structure one could make before they all tumbled down. Concertina books and all books devised from the origami principle are like that. One can make a three-dimensional environment that is able to change its shape while remaining the same form.

The selection of form is conditioned by the nature of the book's contents, and conversely the pattern can condition the concept of the content. In the realm of book art, the book's form and content interact, one influencing the concept of the other. Without sensitivity towards this organic interrelationship, the effectiveness of communication is reduced. In a rare book on the subject, Stephen Gordon (1970) examines the potential of the folding book form in older pupils' learning of graphic sequence, with particular reference to the influence of TV, film, and photojournalism on the structure.

> A book that shows only one page at a time is modest compared to one that grows in size as it opens. A book that has many alternative arrangements is far more sophisticated than the one that can open in only one direction.

The advertising media has put the multidirectional form to good use, much more, in fact, than education has done. Its potential in project work, where diagrams or maps may need to extend in a vertical direction from a horizontally directed book, is considerable (See Diagram 3–13). Not surprisingly, children's picture books have explored this technique effectively and can make good models (see Figure 3–1).

The concertina and associated origami structures are capable of astonishing feats of book design, but within those units another world of invention awaits the book artist. Engineered doors, windows, and pop-ups can transform the inherent imagery of the page and make the book form more like an architectural model (see Diagram 3–14).

The cathedral *is* a story. To walk around a great Gothic cathedral is to enact a spatial

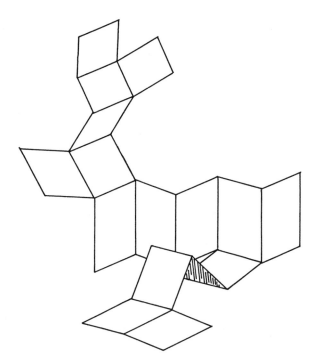

Diagram 3–13.

Figure 3–1. Design for *The Tree House* (by the author) stimulated by *The Oak* by Naomi Russell.

liturgy. In illuminated books of the period, the images are not infrequently contained within an architectural framework (see Figure 3–1).

Diagram 3–14.

Figure 3–2.

All forms of art are so closely connected with life and thought, so bound up with human conditions, habits and customs; so intimately and vivid do they reflect every phase and change of that unceasing movement—the ebb and flow of nature we call history. . . . The story of man is fossilised for us, as it were, or rather preserved, with all its semblance of life and colour, in art and books. The processions of history reaching far back into the obscurity of the forgotten or inarticulate past, is reflected, with all its movement, gold and colour, in the limpid stream of design, that mirror-like, paints each passing phase for us, and illustrates each act in drama. In the language of line and of letters, of symbol and picture, each age writes its own story and character, as page after page is turned in the book of time. —*Walter Crane (1896)*

The best architecture of all periods tells a mythological story; staircases, corridors, rooms, and rooms leading off rooms invite a kinesthetic, symbolic journey into the collective unconscious. The tragedy of so

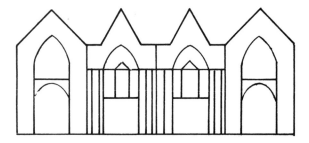

Diagram 3–15. Gothic sequence.

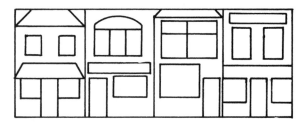

Diagram 3–16. Townscape sequence.

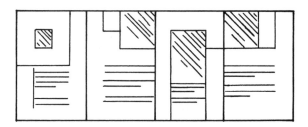

Diagram 3–17. Book design plan.

much book design in our time, like so much architecture and interiors, is that the fashion for minimalism has blocked off our mythological thirst and instinct. Similarly, page after page of unremitting type with no spatial awareness denies the eye's mind its necessity for design. Shape, rhythmic line, and the design of space are human needs. It is not without significance that bookshop browsers flick through illustrated rather than nonillustrated books. We *need* pictures and decoration. They are part of our psychology. An analogy of a well-designed book is landscape gardening—juxtapositions of shapes (flower beds, clumps of bushes), areas of

texture (plants, trees), the restfulness of inactivity (grassed or paved areas). Just a beautiful flower head can transform a brick wall into a visually satisfying design. When teaching children to perceive their own books as a kind of architectural landscape, I use, where possible, arrangements around them like the school and its playground and grassed areas.

This means that a narrative "visualization" is experienced in a whole new dimension than conventional writing processes. There is no need for children to plan a developmental plot in some cerebral way because the book *is* the analogue of the narrative journey. They experience changing situations and events in a visually stimulated sequence. The active book accesses their mental story-making equipment and shapes thoughts into a sequence of dramatic encounters, a visual and tactile experience. One can physically open doors and windows, look through and imaginatively pass through them; bridges can be walked over with the fingers; the forms of things as they appear in real or imagined life can be cut out or popped-up into actual space. Moreover, this framework can interact with the images of

Diagram 3–18 and Diagram 3–19. Hypothetical book designs loosely based on school environment.

words and art so that the processes of narrative development moves into a multiconcept dimension. And all this from one folded piece of paper, a craft knife, and a pencil.

There is a factor here of special relevance. Nearly every teacher experiences the child who writes a three-sentence story and says "I've finished." One of several hundred techniques of literacy education is then brandished at the child in an attempt to prize out a few more words—even, if one is lucky some kind of development and shape to the narrative—before he or she gives up the creative ghost or is lost to disinterest. In the ready-made book of any number of pages, with or without doors and pop-ups, it is impossible for the book artist to say on page two, "I've finished." It has no meaning. The book simply will not allow itself to be left blank. A half-finished book is not a book at all. It is only part of a book. The story, or if it comes to that, writing for any purpose, does not have a definitive structure. It might be crudely described as having a beginning, a middle, and an end, but that formula can be accommodated by a one-sentence story. What the folded book concept does is to stretch the imagination out of its complacency and tells it how to behave, guides it to a goal. And yet when that task is accomplished, the empty book that enabled its contents to happen disappears from view. The contents take complete credit for the whole book, folds and all, because, metaphorically speaking, the walls of the house are no longer visible through the decor.

The psychology of the fold has another function than the dynamism of its image-making plasticity. I cannot recall ever receiving a greetings card that was not folded. Now this can be explained by its necessity to stand up and be displayed; but is this the only reason? The greetings card is like a gift dressed in wrapping paper and tied with a bow. The envelope the card travels in is the tied bow, the fold is the wrapping paper, and the words inside are the gift. We have a desperate need for surprises and the mystery of the unknown. Doors and cupboards and drawers in desks function not only as entries into storage and retrieval systems but as access points into the secret world of the unexpected. As a child I was taken to visit an eccentric couple who lived in a large house by the sea. We were taken on a tour of the house, and all the rooms bar one were made available for our inspection. Later, I made an excuse to go to the bathroom so I could peep through the keyhole of this room. All that I could see was blackness. To this day I speculate what was in there. Fiction for all ages is saturated with doors that lead into that uncompromising unknown. The cover of a greetings card or book is like that; it makes demands to be opened. I try to make children aware of how a cover design can entice an audience to get to the stage of opening the cover of their books.

This mystification and consequent demystification is indigenous to the empty concertina-type book: it begs to be energized with communicating symbols. The empty book is already filled from the moment one possesses it. The challenge to make the unfulfilled book fulfilled unlocks the door into the imagination, for only the book concept holds the key. The book is its own stimulus and few can resist its magnetic power. I have tried various experiments with children in which some compose stories on single unfolded sheets and others work on folded ones. Skills of developmental writing were noticeably higher in the latter. The fold is an invitation into something tantalizingly magical. We enter a book through a fold; without it there is no way in, and once in, no way out without it.

Children targeting an audience with their writing is a contemporary trend. "Publishing" is a much used concept in literacy education, signifying the stage at which the child releases his or her work to the outside world. To all intents and purposes this gestatory externalization is symbolically a book, because in its myriad forms it is the prime way we can communicate cohesive, graphically expressed ideas. How logical it would be if children of all ages conceived writing, from genesis to accomplishment, through the book form, like "real" authors!

The concertina book, for all its potential, is really only where book art begins. By making incisions in the paper base—the origami route—other structural possibilities are possible. Although the cutting patterns are limited, the range of book forms made from them is not. there are two basic routes, one producing portrait books and the other landscape.

The simplest and perhaps most captivating of the portrait form necessitates cutting the two central horizontal panels on the landscape format. Two other portrait books

Diagram 3–20.

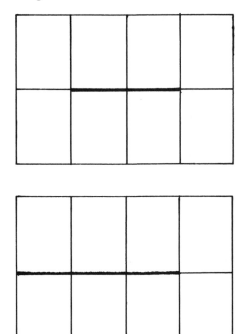

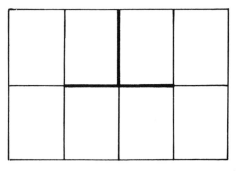

Diagram 3–21.

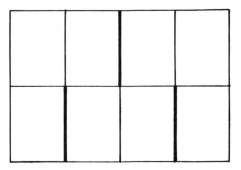

Diagram 3–22.

can be developed from this. One by extending the horizontal cutting by one more panel, and the other by cutting vertically from the center. To make a landscape book, three alternating vertical cuts are made. Other books and folded forms can be produced by cutting patterns, but the ones shown are the most successful and offer the greatest possibilities.

Each of these books introduces a way of thinking peculiar to the form. The young book artist presented with a finished but empty book is faced with the challenge of making it come alive with a structured content. This is a new approach to word and image creativity, for one must design a content to fit a prescribed form. The parameters of literacy education are normally more open-ended; children write without restriction, addressing a plan or goal. The finished product is then given an identity, perhaps a book form, but this is designed to accommodate what has been written. Those in advertising design will be far more familiar with the technique of conceiving content within the definitive area of a folded sheet of paper, for this is the common discipline of their craft. Reducing copy, selecting typeface, arranging visual material within a design concept to fit the two, three, or four folds of a set size and format concentrates the mind wonderfully. With all the book art projects with which I have been involved, children either make themselves, partially or wholly, or are given, a complete book. Conforming to the origami principle they average eight pages. Children are then presented with the task of organizing a definitive sequence of ideas into an illustrated story or project book. Within this foundation there are numerous variations of structure that can add or subtract pages. So, while the discipline of accommodating ideas into a prescribed area is an essential learning experience, there is also the opportunity to reduce or enlarge the plan if the scheme warrants it or if objectives change.

The dimensional size of a book is also a factor. A large-page book can accommodate more data than a small one, but size shouldn't necessarily dictate quantity. Children's picture books are often of large dimensions but few words; illustrations, and the important concept of empty space, predominate the page spreads. Whereas with emerging authors the space words fill will be minimal, the same is not true of artwork, for an illustration can fill a page of any size just as a large sheet of paper on an easel can be "filled" with a painted image. The size factor in children's illustrations needs scrutiny; reluctant image makers can feel less intimidated by drawing on a small scale while more confident pupils could be stultified by the same space. Empty space is an essential part of a book's aesthetic appeal. But there is a difference between a designed emptiness and a book with empty spaces. The concept of designed emptiness is highly sophisticated,

for space can be shaped in the same way as words or illustrations. The reader should only be aware of emptiness when it lacks design; well planned space is real, a kind of positive negative that the searching eye processes as form.

In the basic concertina book of eight pages, page one contains the title. When folded down on the horizontal and folded into the concertina this becomes the front cover, opening to left side page two—the beginning of the book's contents. (In publishing, it is standard practice for left-hand pages to be even numbered and right, odd.) This can be perceived as a half-title page and the beginning of text or a whole page of text. The seven content pages are structured in two main ways: the seven-page or the four-page format.

Diagram 3–23.

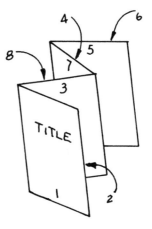

1.   *Seven-page format:* Of the maximum number of seven contents pages, four are arranged on the front folds and three on the back. The final page (8) can be conceived as synopsis, back cover, or end of text.

2.   *Four-page format:* This comprises the front four panels of the book only. The back section is left blank except (possibly) for page six which, in the closed-down book, is in essence the back cover. This back page can become a design area or used for advertising synopsis and logo.

The Eight-Page Book Design Concept

There are as many ways of designing a book as a house. The following diagrams suggest ways of planning the concertina genre. The underlying ideas are applicable, however, to any style of book regardless of size or purpose. To ease scansion, the reversed top line has been realigned with the bottom line.

Progressive book design with children needs a book to itself, and so what I have tried to do is address these aspects as they occur in the school-based work that follows. An apparent dilemma for the children's book art analyst is the sheer volume of categories rising from the page. The written content can be subdivided into a number of categories including structure, clarity of expression, the mechanics of grammar, handwriting. How effectively has the text been constructed to match the book concept? Similarly, illustration comprises appropriateness of imagery,

Diagram 3–24. Four designs utilizing all eight pages.

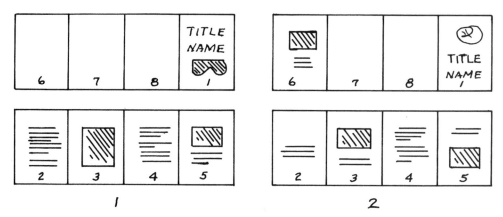

Diagram 3–25. (1) Design showing arrangement of words and images on one side of the book. (2) The contents accommodated on one side of the book but the back cover integrated into the back sequence.

composition, use of line, color relationships, the handling of materials and techniques. Then there is the conceptual interrelationship between the text and illustration. How successfully do they coexist? Does one amplify the meaning of the other? Next there is the area of page design in which one sees the blocks of writing as "shapes" relating to other shapes—illustrations and space. Borders, margins, the lettering of titles, even the placing of the page numbers, all condition the overall visual impression of the whole page, whole double page, and ultimately whole book, including front and (where relevant) back covers. One could systematically analyze every book a child makes in, say, thirty or forty categories. Even if one was so fanatically thorough as to do this diagnostically, it would be impossible to formulate a strategy for concurrently examining each component part. One trains the imaginative and thinking eye to select areas to be processed further—story plot development here, drawing skills there, handwriting, page layout, cover design some time later, when intuition, the teacher's most powerful piece of equipment, suggests the time is right for it. Some children will be born to make books, as some of the

illustrations here testify, but for others it will take years for all these skills to be orchestrated into a holistic book art language reaching into every area of communication. Some skills will develop faster than others and many months of consistent effort may be necessary before any recognizable progress is discernible. What must be safeguarded within book art programs is enthusiasm for the genre. There must be times when inferior work is accepted because to demand rewriting or redrawing would kill the desire to make and create. Conversely, to accept only the best from some pupils secures a higher level of awareness and achievement. (The subject of designing, assessing, and evaluating book art programs for the curriculum are addressed in Part Four.) Teaching is always a fine balancing act between acceptance and insistence.

In my courses for teachers I encourage intuitive understanding. Jean Liedloff is right when she says that we in the West, unlike those in many other parts of the world, no longer trust our instinct. I must confess to being skeptical towards so many of the attitudes towards evaluation today which, far from elucidating curriculum strategies, do the very opposite. So often evaluation is treated like a subject in itself, devoid of sensitivity in what is to be experienced or the true nature of the learning experience. Donald Graves (1983) has shown that the writing process is a partnership between teacher and pupil; that if contextual writing is important for children then it should be important for us not only as teachers but in the wholeness of our lives.

Only through personally experiencing the power of writing to clarify thought, widen our perception of the world around us, and illuminate the journey ahead can we be changed. When we expand the magnitude of writing to the total book concept, to art and design and "a book way of thinking," we are raised to a new and far-reaching level of consciousness. As with our children, not all these innate qualities will emerge at once. It may take years for our drawing or color sensitivity to catch up with our writing, especially if we have brainwashed ourselves into believing that we can't do it.

In my courses for teachers we begin by making basic concertina and origami books, and then, using a narrative concept, structure through words and illustration a simple picture book of our own. For many it is the first time a creative journey has been made since they were students. The ideas I use to develop stories in writing and pictures with children I use with my own teaching colleagues. There is an inevitable degree of self-questioning when they begin their projects, but it is usually a revelation to all participants when, after two or three sessions, they have realized a finished eight-page concertina book. The confidence and knowledge gained from this kind of experience is of more relevance to successful curriculum planning than any preconceived methodology might be.

An understanding of progressive book forms and all they contain, and the capabilities of our children in the two great communication systems *is* the foundation for evaluative judgments. We must learn to trust what we *feel* as being the most accurate forecast of what our children need and how they need it. Decisions must be based on our belief in the creative energy that is inside us, which has carried, and been carried by, the book concept for over a millennium and which will carry us and those we teach to where we should go.

Some Notes on the Reproductions

One of the problems of reproducing artwork, especially on the small scale, is that so much is lost in the process. Yellow can virtually disappear, and delicate pencil work follows the same fate. Areas of subtle tonal work can appear as uneventful masses, and detailed filigree-type draftsmanship, which children seem to indulge in, blur into a nondescript smudge. In an attempt to compensate for this loss, some artwork that I've included has been redrawn in pen to sharpen the imagery or texture that is there but unseen.

Another problem is scale. To make maximum use of space available, the reproduced size of books has been determined on their content rather than their actual size. Thus, a large book with a few sizeable words and images may appear smaller than a small book with tightly packed, minuscule writing. Alas, not many children design their books to be reproduced in books like this! In each case the measurement of children's books (height first, width second) are given after their names. (These are in centimeters first and inches second, and they refer to the dimensions of the closed books.)

Page Arrangements

When laid out flat, many books have their top row of pages head-to-head with the bottom pages, and therefore upside down.

To ease scansion however, books are reproduced in the 3-D format in which they are conventionally read. Sometimes book covers are arranged as one reads them (as first page), and at other times as last page (as they appear in the logical sequence of folded pages when flat). As much as possible the design arrangement has been selected to present each book in the best possible way.

Page Numbering

Earlier it was stated that it is a publishing convention to number left side pages as even numbers. However, for young children to start a book on page two is something of an irrational system. For this reason some books illustrated here number the first left page as page one.

part two

chapter 4

The Concertina Explicated

The Concertina Concept

There are two important aspects that the book form brings to bear on writing. One is the organization into a finite number of pages and the other is the illustration/design ambience. Some children naturally illustrate their stories, others display no recognizable need to do so. The objective of producing an illustrated book clearly states the nature of the task and the process involved. From the beginning of the activity, children's thinking in the book planning stages is influenced by the books they read and look at. But successful book design cannot be reduced to that experience alone. "Lilly the Litter Bug" (see Figure 4–7, page 54) exemplifies feeling for the book concept that is personal and intuitive. When word and image fit the book as comfortably as this it cannot be solely explained as the skill to rationally plan what will go where and how to spin out a yarn to fit a set number of pages.

The illustrated book has come down to us as an expression of our humanity, an innate ability to communicate through words and images and to empathize with folded paper. What I am saying—and it is wrong to dismiss such ideas as "romantic"—is that this organization of words into a meaningful shape, of balancing pictures and words into a sculptured form in the round—for that is what a concertina book is—is holistically organic. Some children seem to have it from the beginning, others acquire it through the intuitive leadership of the insightful teacher.

Some of the books reproduced here are the result of a planned sequence of development; others are the product of more or less unrelated projects. I admire the dedication of teachers pioneering new ideas like these, especially when they themselves are learning concurrently with the children and burdened with an overloaded curriculum.

A proportion of the work shown here is the product of the commissioning scheme described in the Introduction. The concept of these books is discussed in our monthly consultations. Processing takes the form of some school-based activity, but mostly the work is done at home and largely unsupervised. The books are not therefore the consequence of considerable teacher-oriented input but rather a self-motivated endeavor. The advantage of this approach is that one can observe behavioral traits as children respond to the book challenge. What traits are recognizable? Do children have an innate design awareness? What do they find the hardest challenges?

One thing clear is that children perceive the book form in many different ways. There are variations in the delegation of writing and illustration to the page spreads. Some children limit their stories to the four front folds of the concertina while others continue on to the reverse side. The unwritten-on back pages are left blank, colored in with decorations, or contain visual subject matter relevant to the book's theme. One might deduce from this that for some the book serves the needs of the author, and that others serve the needs of the book. The content of some books lack page awareness: children write with the same insensitivity to the page surface that exercise books encourage. Yet scanning these examples it is evident that for many emergent book artists there is a consciousness that a bond exists between the idea of a story and the idea of a book; that when you make a story to go into a book you must respect the right of the book to lay down its own rules of conduct.

What I am eager to avoid is suggesting mechanistic structures and systematic processes that will produce specified attainment targets. Rather I pose the question: What does children's creativity in the book arts tell us about what they are communicating, how they communicate it, and how they might communicate it more effectively?

With so many different aspects of the book arts all demanding attention, it is problematic to place in any logical sequence an appraisal of children's work. What I have done is to organize the sections in relation to paper technology book-form design. The aim here is to see if the book's "architectural form" significantly influences how it is conceived in its entirety. Flat-topped, basic concertina books start the sequence, and this is followed by progressively more complex structures.

The Concordant Concertina

The four-fold concertina, the most basic of all book forms, has already been described and needs no further description here.

Naomi was given the folded concertina and asked if she would like to make a book (see Figure 4–1). She thought for a moment

Figure 4–1. *Red Riding Hood* Naomi (5) (20 x 16 cm; 8 x 6 in).

and then started to draw Red Riding Hood (1) and the wolf (2). When asked what she was going to do next she replied, "the story": "This is little red riding hood" (3), "this is the wolf" (4). Both the visual and written forms are sequenced but separate from one another.

Scott made a four-fold concertina, (See Figure 4–2). A rectangular template was used to make a one-centimeter border to each page.

Q.   Where did the idea of ghosts in Scotland come from?
A.   I had seen a film on TV which had ghosts and castles and so I thought I would use them in my book.
Q.   You are also the main character in it, aren't you?
A.   Yes.
Q.   How did you prepare your book? Did you make it in draft form first?
A.   I did most of it at home. I started to write it in draft but I wanted to get on with the book so I then wrote straight into it.
Q.   How did you know what to write on each page?
A.   Somehow you seem to know when there's enough.
Q.   And you didn't want too much so that you had enough room for the illustrations?
A.   Yes, I had to write outside the borders to get it all in.

In the continuation of book one (see Figure 4–3), there are several noticeable differences.

1.   There is a greater consciousness of the page—blocks of narration fit more aesthetically into the space provided.
2.   The imagery of the artwork is more strategically placed in the picture area, partly because its proportion of the page space has been reduced and so the subject matter is necessarily more specific.
3.   I asked Scott why in this book he printed the words rather than writing cursive. From his reply it was clear that he was becoming much more aware of an audience of young children for his book: they wouldn't be able to read his writing—hence individually drawn letters
4.   In comparing both books, (a) the text of the latter is sharper, more succinct than the former and (b) the second reflects a real feeling for "total page design."

Q.   Scott, you're now on your third sequalized book.
A.   Yes. I just want to keep writing more about the same things.

Figure 4–2. *Ghosts of the Scottish Moor* **Scott (8) (16 x 11 cm; 6 x 4 in).**

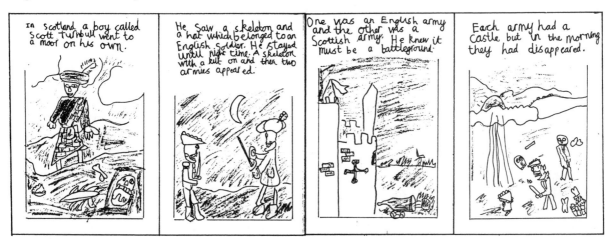

Figure 4–3. *The Ghosts of the Scottish Moor Come Back* Scott
(16 x 11 cm; 6 x 4 in).

Q.   And you've filled both front and back of the book.
A.   I wanted to carry on writing at home, but I didn't have another book to work in so I carried on on the back.
Q.   You're now using full pages of writing and illustration. Why?
A.   I wanted to write more and do bigger pictures so my Mum said why don't you do it like that.
Q.   You've gone back to joined up letters again. Why?
A.   Yes, I got bored with writing with single letters. It took too long.
Q.   Are there more books to follow?
A.   Yes, at least three more.

Scott is highly self-motivated with above average communication skills. Yet when I met him those skills had not been harnessed and developed. The book form, with its facility of *ad infinitum* continuity, is just what he needed to project himself forward. He is able to slip the small book(s) into his school bag and work on them when the opportunity presents itself at both school and home. As each book comprises only eight sides he is under no obligation to write at length, yet this freedom produces the opposite effect—the compilation of episodic story books!

Some interesting issues are raised by his comments. One is the importance of embracing parents in book art activities. Scott's mum has taken a personal interest in his books, and her intelligent eye is helping him (and perhaps herself) to perceive the potential of the book's adaptability. Comparing his three books evidences the extent of his development in just three to four weeks. Another observation concerns his attitude in producing a book for a younger audience. Scott found the task of printing each word for emergent readers restricting. He needed to return to his cursive writing style to meet his own needs and development.

Collaborative Writing

These books represent collaborative writing projects with six-year-old children. The class teacher, a book arts enthusiast for several years, found herself moving from solo to interactive activities.

At first I thought that two or more children making a book together would be less effective, almost a dilution of individually

Scott and John went back to the moor. As dusk came a mist came over the moor. They saw the big castle with the big wooden door opening with a creaky sound.

They ran inside and saw suits of armour, a stags head mounted on the oak panelled wall, plastered ceilings with carvings of lions and shields, portraits in gold frames, tapestries of huting scenes and stone floors. A white hooded ghost with a beckoning finger came towards them down a long hall.

They retreated up some steps to the top of the tower. They looked out of the window and saw the mist over the loch. They heard the grass rustling, some bagpipes and a drum. In the distance they saw a skeleton playing the bagpipes and another beating the drum.

Out of the mist over the loch came a huge neck with a head turning slowly from side to side. When the dawn came the ghosts and the monster vanished.

THE LOCH NESS MONSTER By Scott Turnbull

Figure 4–4. *The Loch Ness Monster* (Scott) (16 x 11 cm; 6 x 4 in).

produced books. Children became so attached to them and want to take them with them everywhere they go.

She found that ground rules had to be made to avoid an unbalanced work load: "It is essential that the groups discuss and brainstorm story plots, but only one child can write on the page at a time." So one rule was that each of the three children (the groups usually comprised three) would be responsible for some part of the text. This applied equally to the illustrations, title page design, and

miscellaneous design work. The books then became part of the school's book art collection. In every case, the trios were of mixed ability. Guy, a child with learning difficulties, joined Emma and Sean. He sat watching the other two busily preparing the page-by-page structure and gradually he contributed by making suggestions. By the time the four-fold concertina had been turned over he was actively engaged. On page seven he felt confident enough to provide the page illustration. "This was a great thrill for him," said his teacher, "and stimulated him directly to make 'Mr. Guy's Toy Shop'—a seven-page concertina story book with all the writing by him." All the illustrations are drawn on separate pieces of paper and glued into the book. The illustration shape is drawn around

so that the writer knows how much space is available for the text. In an early example from these collaborative enterprises, the pages are clearly defined as top—illustration, bottom—text. This was prescribed by the teacher.

Figure 4–5. *The Bear and the Sun* Hannah, Jenny, Chris (23 x 16 cm; 9 x 6 in).

A great deal of discussion went on in the beginning stages of a new book. They disagreed. They fell out. But in the end they knew they had to find a way to work together.

One hour every two days was allocated for each group to work on their book art.

The story in Figure 4–5 is about a bear called Barnett who was fat but who made friends with the sun, who kept him warm when he was outside and went shopping. Chris took charge of the first four pages of writing, Hannah the first two illustrations, and Jenny the following two. Over on the back, Jenny took over the writing with Hannah contributing, but mainly providing the illustrations. Chris's awareness of page design from books he had seen and read influenced him to write in four regularly spaced lines. Even when these become irregular towards the end of the first side, the fourth line is still placed at the base of the page. The illustrations are iconic in character, environments being contextually minimal.

About three months later, "The Greedy Bear" was produced (Figure 4–6). This is a summary of the plot:

> Once there was a bear called Bill. He was very greedy indeed. He ate so much that one of the buttons of his coat fell off. Eventually he found it and decided to have a celebration. He invited several guests including God who said to Bill "I have come to say do what you like. Be fat not thin it doesn't matter." Bill was so pleased at God's comment about him that he never cried again.

Hannah has developed from being primarily an illustrator to including writing as well. The story is more lively, the construction better organized, and letter forms more confidently drawn, meandering freely about the page to accentuate meaning. The overall visual communication techniques have moved on several stages. Important words like "celaibraitson" are visually expressed. When God speaks, it is an explosive "Hello" that signifies his status. Illustrations are arranged freely on the page and become integrated into

Figure 4–5 continued.

once there was a Bear called Bill he was very greedy indeed he lived in a big house and he had a big car and he had a red wache—cook. one day he went for a walk in the medows it was a very hot day he sat down to rest and he ate some grass

and he ate so much grass that one of his buttons fell off. He was so sad he searched and searched the next Day he got up and got redy.

He went to the medow that he was in the Day before and he found the button and he

had a CELAIBRA

and he inveied lots of bears. and the rabbit from next door. and most of all he invited God. the next day he had the CELAIBRAIEION, and all His fraiends came but one that one was God.

Five-year-olds on a book making project.

Figure 4–6. *The Greedy Bear*
Charlotte, Hannah
(23 x 16 cm; 9 x 6 in).

a richly decorated scenario. Their visual content contains information pertinent to the text; middle and far grounds appear for the first time.

A few weeks later Hannah, working with two new partners, produced the book "Lilly the Litter Bug" (Figure 4–7). It begins like this:

One year ago there was a litter bug called Lilly the litter bug, and she lived in very very clen warter. She was very ugly and evry day she ware a very dirty brown dress. . . .

The text, illustrations, and design tasks were evenly shared and some pages bear three

Figure 4–7.
Lilly the Litter Bug
Hannah, Michael, Hayley
(23 x 16 cm; 9 x 6 in).

names, showing just how integrated the corporate spirit had become. The two previous books had been inspired by a classroom display of teddy bears and this one developed out of anti-litter posters the class had made for display in local shops. The growing consciousness of the page concept has partly come about through the use of card templates (two centimeters smaller than the page), providing a measured border to the pages. Professional writing techniques have been observed in their story books and incorporated into their work, for example, using ellipses to hold the reader's attention as they turn the page: "and popped it on his . . . nose" (pages 2/3). Important words like 'Ideer' are once again enlarged and colored in (page 3), as in the advertising media. The sentence construction and the word forms that hold them are generally improving. The textual invention remains high and is delightfully spontaneous. Poor Lilly is disliked by everyone because she smells. People even carry clothespins to put on their noses when they meet her. In desperation she attempts to escape:

I will dig a path throw the payfment to the sea and to a island in the sea and then no one will know wher I am and no one will be . . . abel to smell me . . . on the other hand . . . the fish . . . might . . .

But even the fish put clothespins on their noses. So she went home where she had a revelation: "I've got it. I am going to have a bath." So she had a bath and a new hairdo. And everybody loved her.

The illustrations develop organically out of the text. The last one shows Lilly blissfully singing in the bathtub as bubbles rise around her. One of the most striking features of this book is the evidence of the "psychology of the fold." Each page holds a distinctive story progression.

- *Page 1:*   description of Lilly
- *Page 2:*   man defining Lilly's smell
- *Page 3:*   Lilly has an idea
- *Page 4:*   description of her idea
- *Page 5:*   sequential account of journey
- *Page 6:*   revelation
- *Page 7:*   realization

Figure 4–7 continued.

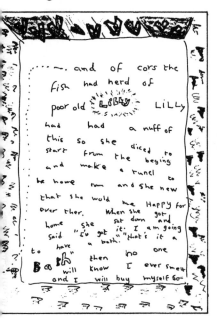

The last page, in which we see Lilly under the hair dryer against a portrait on the wall captioned "The old me," is a model of text/illustration asymmetrical balance. The page is a total concept without an inactive square centimeter. This is one example (one could draw many more from this book) in which the page/fold/book concept has had direct influence on the overall communication construction.

By carefully selecting the composition of each group, strengths can be exploited and weaknesses supported: "Some children are great at improvising stories," said their teacher,

> so I place them with those who are more reticent. Keen illustrators inspire those less inclined to draw. An enthusiastic writer—someone who loves making the shapes of words on paper—stimulates those who would normally avoid writing at all costs to want to do it. . . . But most of all it is the book itself which is the driving force behind all that these children do.

Concertina Exotica

For some children it is the miniscule character of some books that entices the imagination into action. It is increasingly popular for publishers to print miniversions of successful children's picture books. In my collection of concertina books I have one with a cover no more than two centimeters, which I once showed to a group of children I was working with. Although books of largish dimension had been prepared for their use, it was intimate "palm-held" books they were determined to make. I rapidly folded miniscule eight-page books, and Catherine's book (Figure 4–8) is typical of the sensitivity, beauty, and quality of text and illustration that was produced on a few afternoons in a city classroom.

> One day Anna was playing in her sandpit. She was making a road to go to the King and Queen's castle. When just then she saw a box. It was not very big. Anna lifted the lid and looked inside. . . .

Figure 4–8. *The Little Sand People* **Catherine (10) (6 x 6 cm; 2 x 2 in.)**

  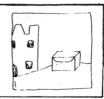

Figure 4–8 continued.

She said of her thirty-page book: "Once I'd started the book I just didn't want to stop."

The Concertina Explored

Transforming the top edge of a concertina by cutting a contour changes the meaning that can be derived from the book form. To explore the contour, fold a sheet of paper on the vertical; fold again, then open the sheet and press flat (see Diagram 4–1). Now improvise a landscape cutting pattern across the center of the sheet, horizontally. It is best to use a cutter for this task because by doing so the paper is left flat on the table and the form is cut just as if it was drawn by a pencil. (Experiment by cutting shapes on pieces of wastepaper, as in Diagram 4–2.)

Cutting is like handwriting: we all have a different way of holding the instrument and using it to make a mark. You will learn with practice the most successful way of using it to suit your own style. Unlike a pencil, the cutter cannot simply meander its way across the sheet guided by your hand. One must learn the gymnastic technique of turning and twisting one's arm, wrist, and fingers so that the tool follows the trajectory of the pattern being cut. Whereas a pencil can move freely up and down on a sheet of paper, if you try that with a cutter you will hack the paper to shreds. A cutter must be pulled *downwards* along its cutting edge and one must therefore follow that direction whatever the desired shape. It is a paper technology skill worth having.

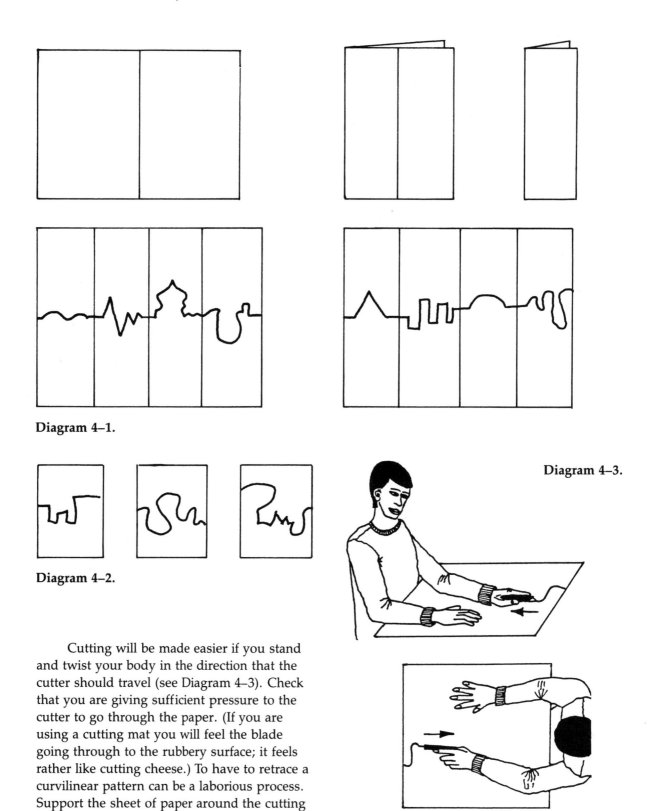

Diagram 4–1.

Diagram 4–2.

Diagram 4–3.

Cutting will be made easier if you stand and twist your body in the direction that the cutter should travel (see Diagram 4–3). Check that you are giving sufficient pressure to the cutter to go through the paper. (If you are using a cutting mat you will feel the blade going through to the rubbery surface; it feels rather like cutting cheese.) To have to retrace a curvilinear pattern can be a laborious process. Support the sheet of paper around the cutting

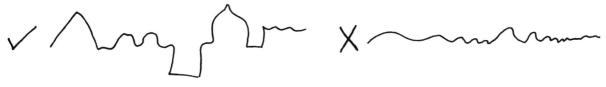

Diagram 4–4.

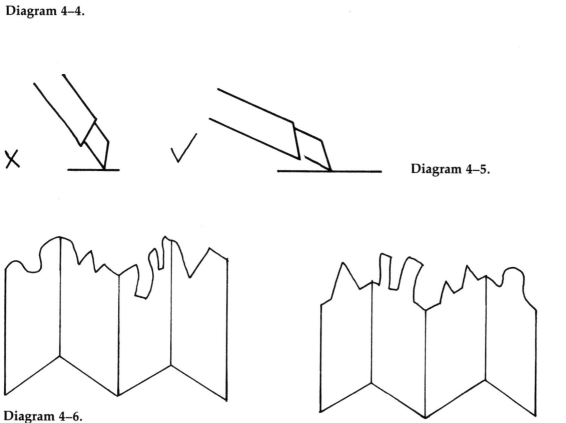

Diagram 4–5.

Diagram 4–6.

area with your free hand. It goes without saying that it should not be placed *beneath* the direction the blade is travelling!

To give variety to your contour, vary the design of the improvisation (see Diagram 4–4). Contrast curved forms with angular ones, spikey shapes with balloon-shaped ones.

If you tear the paper you are probably either cutting at an angle that does not follow the flow of the cutter, or you are holding it at too sharp an angle (see Diagram 4–5). When the sheet has been dissected, concertina both halves and stand them vertically by angling the pages (Diagram 4–6). You have now produced two contour books for the price of one! You will see later how each one has its own unique story to tell.

Cutting centrally on the landscape format is the sturdiest design. Travelling too far to top or bottom of the sheet makes weak and flimsy forms and an aesthetically unbalanced design. But there are exceptions (see Diagram 4–7). There may be thematic projects when wide contrasts of proportion are necessary, for

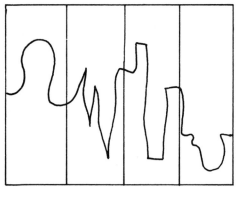

Diagram 4–7.

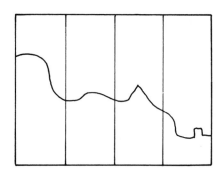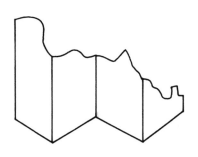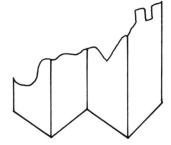

Diagram 4–8. The folding orientation.

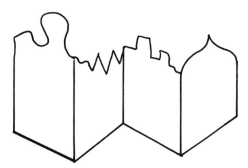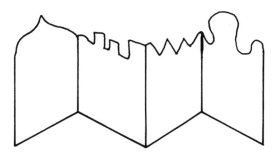

Diagram 4–9. Contour Cover.

example an ascending or descending form; but even here avoid shapes that are narrow or elongated (see Diagram 4–8).

Concertina contours can also be folded in two directions. Each half will then comprise a different pattern from the other (see Diagram 4–9).

As children become more dexterous with contour books it will become evident to them that the shape made for page one is also that of the cover (on the reverse side). This should be taken into account when designing the contours because some shapes will be more visually satisfying than others (see Diagram 4–10).

The left and right vertical ends of the book can be embraced in the overall cutting design as well (see Diagram 4–11).

If you prefer to use scissors to cut the contour (or if children have developed sufficient scissor-cutting skills) draw out a rough outline and then cut to that design (see Diagram 4–12). One technique perfected by the Chinese for making cutout silhouettes is a nice one to practice here. Instead of trying to follow the contours of the drawn line, swing the paper with your free hand so that you are always cutting in a straight direction and the

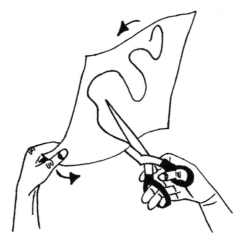

Diagram 4–12. Using scissors.

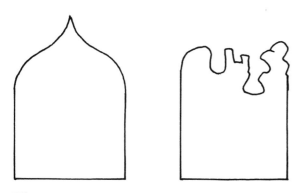

Diagram 4–10.

Diagram 4–11. Vertical contours.

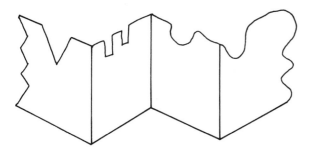

paper does the moving. This is another "dance for the hand" rhythmical exercise that holistically fits the whole concertina concept.

Stories for Contours

I have seen so many teachers and their children at work making stories from contour concertina books that it is difficult to resist taking up the rest of this book describing them. Not all children respond to the contours with wonderfully evocative story plots. Some I have worked with take to it as a birthright and can see a dozen different images in a shape, whereas others seem unable to identify the shape of a tree. For most, however, some shapes are instantly recognizable as buildings, palaces, heads, the sun, while other shapes require discussion to arrive at identification.

After a course for teachers at which I had been singing the praises of contour books as a way into literacy development, a clearly disappointed teacher of nursery-age children rang me to say that the contour books she had spent all evening and half the night making just didn't trigger a response from her children at all. I asked her if she wanted her money back and she laughed, but clearly intentions and responses don't necessarily harmonize. Now it might be that weeks of being surrounded by other children's contour books have to pass before one morning, as from nowhere, a child makes a convincing one of his or her own. But even regardless of the direct stimulatory response, children love the unusual outline along the top of the book, and that in itself can trigger the desire to write and draw in one, regardless of the contour shape. Here are two ways in which the contour book form was used with children:

Example 1

A teacher of five- and six-year-old children cuts a simple concertina contour book. She then discussed with them what the shapes suggested (see Diagram 4–13). A story was then improvised by the group.

Q. What shall we begin our story with?
A. A hill, no a hat.
Q. How many children want a hill . . . or hat? That's about 20 of you want a hat, so a hat it will be. Who is wearing the hat?
A. The old man, a wizard, a giant . . .
Q. So why was the wizard wearing a hat?
A. To make spells.
Q. And what spell was he working on? Let's look at the next shape.
A. It's his house.
Q. But he was in his house at the beginning of the story, so where else could it be?
A. A mountain.
Q. Is it a big or small mountain?
A. A very big mountain.
Q. And what is the spell to do with the mountain?
A. (Several ideas, but finally) The wizard made a spell to make the mountain happy.
Q. Why was the mountain sad?
A. Because it was lonely.
Q. Let's look at the next outline. What's this?
A. It's icicles.
Q. But how can we fit icicles into the story?
A. The mountain was very cold.
Q. Yes, and are there other things we can see in these shapes. Is it like the previous shape?
A. Yes—they're little mountains.

Q. And how does that fit in with the story?
A. The wizard made a spell so that lots of mountains would be friends.
Q. Oh, that's a lovely idea! And the last shape . . .
A. It's a house.
Q. But there are two shapes?
A. Two houses.
Q. And how does that fit in with the story?
A. The wizard went home. All the mountains had a party. It's a castle on the mountain.
Q. So most of you like the idea of a mountain party, so what could these two shapes be? What kinds of things do you eat at parties?
A. Jellies.
Q. And what else? Not round, but flat things?
A. Cakes and sandwiches.

This abbreviated transcript shows how the teacher formulated and orchestrated a contour story with children. Had the book been cut so the order of shapes was reversed (see Diagram 4–14), a totally different story would have emerged: 1. A tall building 2. caught on fire 3. All the snow melted on a nearby mountain and put the fire out, 4. but it also made a great lake of water.

Some narrative constructs fit the contour shapes more easily than others. There are times when it will take a great deal of imaginative invention from both teacher and child to make a story work. But as the above transcript shows, provided the forms are reasonably universal in visually symbolic terms, a great variety can be brainstormed from them. Indeed, the problem is often less what to put in and more what is to be left out. The role of this teacher to help children through the plot invention is significant, but not in an obtrusive way. The developing story must always grow from the children's ideas, but with the teacher carefully holding the shape together. It is no accident that those teachers who develop contour book schemes most successfully are those who encourage story improvisations on a regular basis with their children.

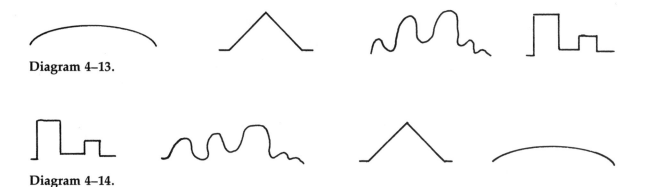

Diagram 4–13.

Diagram 4–14.

In the early stages of narrative experiments of this kind, it might be wise to make books using the story that has been created orally en masse. This means they can concentrate on a personal realization of the narrative. The daunting prospect of making a large number of books the same can be eased by using the multiple cutting technique: hold three sheets of paper together with clips and cut the required pattern through them simultaneously. As you grow in cutting skills and confidence, this will become easier than you can at first imagine. After using identical contour books to gain familiarity with the concept, you can make a variety of book shapes so that pupils can select shapes of their choice and ultimately cut (or ask to have cut) a pattern of their own design. Four-page sequences will inevitably become inadequate for some children, and so the reverse three pages will be explored for development. This creates new challenges for the book artist because the contour on one side of the concertina will take on new meaning on the other.

Example 2

In this contour game with eight-year-olds, the teacher made outline shapes on the board, which the class then improvised into a corresponding story. A development of this was for the class to develop a story simultaneously to the teacher's linear forms drawn on the board. There was great excitement as every attempt was made to identify the shape with a narrative, sequential meaning before a new shape was drawn (see Diagram 4–15).

Diagram 4–15.

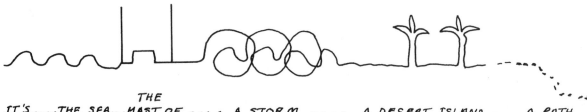

IT'S .... THE SEA ... MAST OF .... , A STORM .... A DESERT ISLAND .... A PATH
THE
A SHIP

A group contour improvisation in progress.

The children were then given four-fold concertina books and invited to draw an outline along the top. They could be asked to improvise or to use a preconceived outline of a planned narrative. Either way there is a challenge. In the first option the authors have to make a story to fit the shape; in the second, a four-part story has to be invented and a shape drawn for each part. The contour is then cut out by scissors and processed into a total book.

In Amy's book "Stories" (see Figure 4–9), the four sections are identified with familiar images, but not sequentialized: 1. Little Red Riding Hood, 2. The Three Bears 3. Treasure Island, 4. In the park. The artwork was drawn first and the writing, with the aid of the teacher, second.

Elliot's book is both sequential and developmental (see Figure 4–10). The image of his house was conceived regardless of the first contour form.

Elliot: This is my house and me (referring to first page).
Teacher: And what could you make this shape at the top of the page into?
E. It's a tree in my garden (he draws tree).
T. We have a space at the bottom of the page. What could go in there?
E. My paddling pool (he draws in paddling pool with his Mum filling it with a hose).
T. What can we make this shape into (referring to second page)? It's like a house but

Figure 4–9. *Stories,* **Amy (5). "This is Little Red Riding Hood's House (1). This is me (pointing to face in contour) and the three bears (2). This is Treasure Island (3). This is a duck in a park (4)."**

Figure 4–10. *My House* **Elliot (5) (22 cm x 15 cm; 9 x 6 in).**

you've already drawn your house. What else could it be?

E. It's my garage (he draws cars in garage contour).

T. Now we've still got the bottom part of the page with nothing in it. What could be there?

E. I don't know.

T. Well, what's around your house? Are there trees or shops?

E. It's over there (he points out of the classroom window to the houses adjacent to the school playground).

T. So what can you see when you look out of your window?

E. The school.

T. and . . . ?

E. Children playing in the playground.

T. Anything else?

E. Trees (he draws the three objects into the page area).

T. Now what can we see in the next shape (page three)?

E. (pause)

T. What do you like doing at home best?

E. Helping Mummy cook.

T. Have you helped her recently?

E. Yes, I made a cake.

T. So what could you put in the shape?

E. The oven (he draws oven in contour form).

T. What else in your kitchen?

E.   Cupboards, a fridge.
T.   Is there anything on the walls of your kitchen?
E.   Cupboards on the walls.
T.   So draw them in (he draws in the kitchen below the oven).
T.   Now this last shape is what (page four)?
E.   A duck.
T.   Now how can we fit a duck into a story about Elliot's house?
E.   He goes for a walk with Mummy into the park and sees a duck (draws duck into contour form).
T.   What else could you see in the park?
E.   Swings and animals (draws swings, animals).

These book art sessions were organized around a red table, which is designated as the writing area and accommodates eight children. The daily cyclical permutations ensure that every child spends some time here. The teacher's technique is to perambulate the group, discussing each book's progress individually. Elliot spent about thirty minutes on each page and took two to three days to complete the book. The above transcript was spread over a two hour, three day period. What is particularly important to observe is the interaction between teacher and child. Left to Elliot's devices, the book would probably have gone no further than the images of home and "me" on page one. Even if the four sequential stages of house/garage/kitchen/park had been processed with images it is questionable that the in-depth conceptualization would have happened without the teacher's tireless questioning. The detailed analysis of the house environment and kitchen interior shows the readiness of Elliot to recall so much stored experience. And this book form is the perfect vehicle to enable the transformation of experience into the sequencing process. He has moved to a new plane in his ability to "make a model of reality." The sensitive awareness of the teacher in drawing out from the child the full potential of each page's spatial meaning cannot be overestimated. A few seconds of discussion at developmental points through the conceptualizing period can make a world of difference to the pace of children's progress. It is a team—child/teacher/book—effort.

In another school, a class of older children had been researching a project into trees and made drawings and paintings of them from life. Joanne's finished product exemplifies the related book project that followed. She was given a strip of paper (60 x 23 cm; 24 x 9 inches) and drew on it the outline of a wooded land-scape (see Diagram 4–16). The contour was cut out by scissors and the artwork completed, leaving a space on the extreme right side for the title. The strip was concertina-folded into five areas. On the front side of the book she decided to allocate writing to pages two through four and artwork to pages one and five. The artwork was roughed in, the drafted story written in next, and finally the colorwork and title page completed.

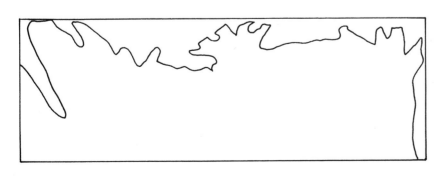

Diagram 4–16.

A Noise in the Night **Joanne (11) (23 x 14 cm; 9 x 5 in).**

Variations of Paper Engineering

There are several additional ways of engineering a contour to a concertina book. This first technique is taken a stage further in Diagram 4–17.

1. Fold a largish landscape-orientated sheet in half and in half again on the vertical.
2. Draw a line across the horizontal center, *but do not fold.*
3. Cut simple forms in the area above the line in the four sections. Ensure that there is a gap between the engineering and the vertical folds.

4. Gently fold the top half down over the bottom half of the sheet.

This folding technique avoids creasing the raised forms, which would spoil the appearance of the raised contour. A special feature of this book form is that two entirely different forms exist on the front and back sides because the negative area creates a mirror image of the engineered form.

In Amee's ingenious story book, seven semi-circular contours have been identified with round objects and a narrative sequence constructed around them.

Diagram 4–17.

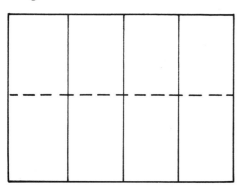

1/2

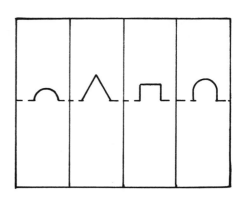

3

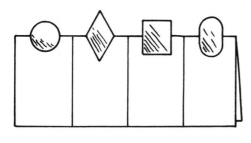

4

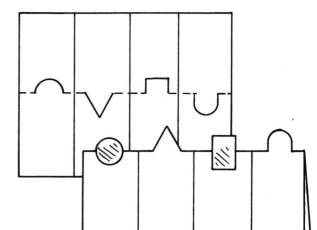

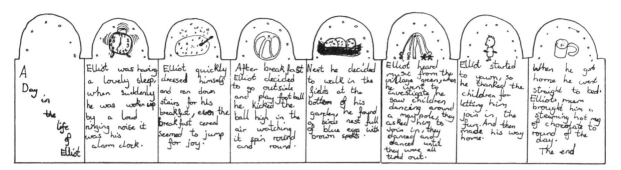

Figure 4–11. *A Day in the Life of Elliot* Amee (10)
(10 cm x 5 cm; 4 x 2 in).

- *Alarm clock:* Elliot is asleep, wakes up
- *Bowl of cereal:* has his breakfast
- *Ball:* goes out to play
- *Birds' eggs:* sees birds' eggs in his garden

- *Maypole:* he hears music, sees children dancing on the village green
- *Yawning mouth:* he begins to feel tired
- *Round mug:* goes home to bed and a hot drink

Bill and the Vampire Nick (12) (34 x 16 cm; 13 x 6 in).

Her process entailed doing the illustrations first, then drafting the text, and finally writing the text into the book. She described the ease with which she carried out her round-object theme: "I thought of a clock first and getting up in the morning and the rest of the round things seemed to come to me as I decided what to do next."

Nick is a talented author and illustrator who had made several books prior to the one I've included, and is now in high school. In an attempt to foster his book art skills I continue to commission him, through letters, to make books:

Dear Nick,

I hope things are going well in your new school. I have recently made some new style books and I wonder if you would like to have a go working on one? I am sending it along in the envelope so see what you make of it.

Best wishes

What you see in the photograph is the first four pages of the book he made at home. The humorously macabre imagery that typifies children approaching adolescence can so easily fall into a quasi-cartoon style, but Nick's narrative, illustration, and design has a degree of sophistication that avoids clichés.

The "turned-in" concertina

Another way to mold the contour of a double-fold concertina is by turning in the top edge. No paper is wasted by cutting and the folded forms help to strengthen and support the contour. It is surprising how many shapes can be made from the permutations of vertical, horizontal, and diagonal folds.

In Diagram 4–18 vertical folds are employed to create a cityscape, though this technique works well on a wide variety of themes.

Diagram 4–18.

1

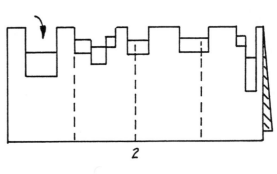

2

3

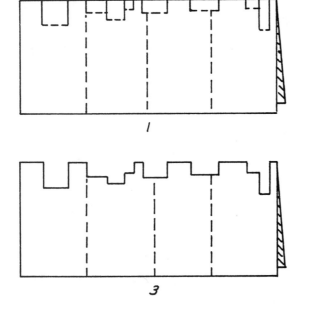

4

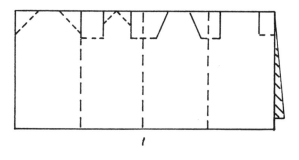

1

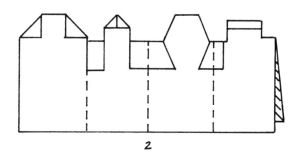

2

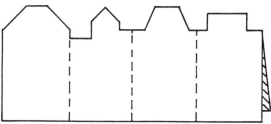

INTERNALIZE ENGINEERED SECTIONS AS
ABOVE.

3

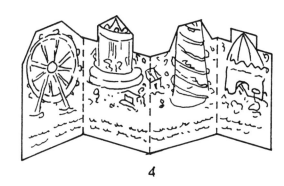

4

Diagram 4–19.

1. Fold concertina on landscape horizontal. Cut patterns of vertical lines (with scissors or cutter) through doublefold.
2. Fold selected double-page vertical areas down (forward) to represent a theme.
3. Fold back engineered parts to former positions again and fold *inward* to center of horizontal fold.
4. The book is now ready for thematic, textual, and visual development.

Vertical and diagonal folds can be used together to vary the shapes (see Diagram 4–19).

1. Fold concertina on landscape horizontal. Cut pattern of vertical lines and crease selected diagonals.

2. Fold vertical areas forward and fold diagonals forward.
3. Internalize the engineered sections as before.
4. Develop theme.

For special effects, combinations of techniques can be explored (see Diagram 4–20).

1. Fold paper on landscape vertical *only*. Draw central horizontal line. Sketch out forms, with one major form (e.g., cathedral form) on or near landscape horizontal.
2. Cut out the major shape.
3. Fold concertina on landscape *excluding* the cutout shape. Cut verticals and crease diagonals for other forms.

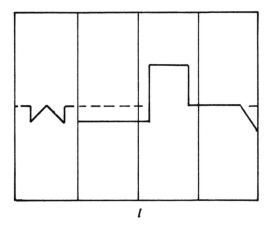

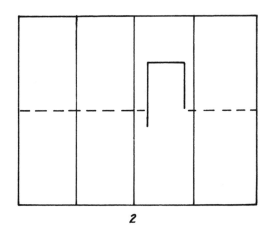

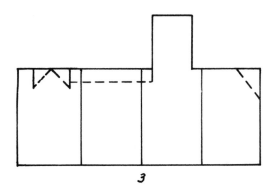

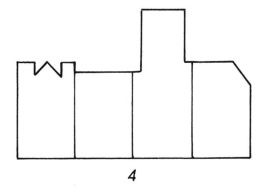

Diagram 4–20.

4.   Fold down forms, raise again, and internalize as before.

There must be thousands of thematic variations. A group project on bridges shows one variation. The class made and tested bridges of many kinds and researched them historically and scientifically, each subgroup concentrating on one particular type of bridge. One of their tasks was to design and make a bridge concertina book. Simulations were prepared on used duplicating paper, and their teacher demonstrated the basic cutting and folding techniques. On other pieces of waste-paper the subgroups explored specified bridge forms (e.g., suspension, cantilever). When the forms had been mastered, the finished models were engineered on thin card.

Chris and John's bridges (see photographs) were planned to have artwork on one side and writing on the other. Other design strategies are:

1.   Text along base of four-fold concertina
2.   Contour-text following outline of bridge
3.   Bridge conceived as artwork model and description prepared in accompanying booklet.

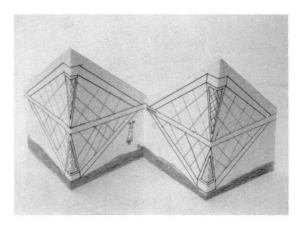

Tower Bridge Chris (11) (16 x 11 cm; 6 x 4 in).

Forth Bridge John (11) (16 x 11 cm; 6 x 4 in).

Diagram 4–21.

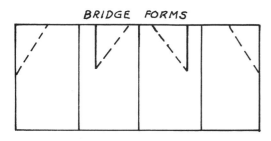

BRIDGE FORMS

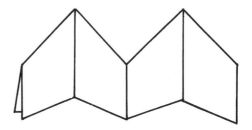

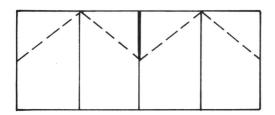

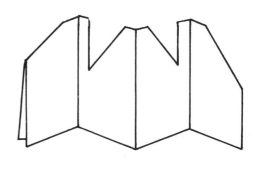

chapter 5

The Concertina Expanded

Doors, Windows, and Narratives

Engineered doors, windows, and openings in a concertina book introduce to children a whole new way of conceiving narratives, communication strategies, and sequencing in general (see Diagram 5–1). Whereas contours can be cut with scissors, engineered doors need the use of a cutter. However, scissors can be used when there is a door on a contour.

The shape given to a door suggests the house or location to which it belongs, and those who are—or could be—inside (see Diagram 5–2). Similarly, windows define or suggest the nature of the dwelling and who or what is in the interior (see Diagram 5–3).

In *single-sheet books*, doors and windows open out to nothing. Yet children, through the power of imagination, "see" a room or forest through the aperture. The hinged form has the creative thrust to suggest spatial meaning, not necessarily the reality of such a concept.

In *double-sheet books*, doors and windows can actually look into an interior or out to an exterior. This is challenging for the book artist and enticing for the viewer. Who can resist opening the doors and windows and seeing what is beyond? The easiest way to imagine this area is to draw the outline through the aperture, to open up the concertina to its whole-sheet size, and to draw the appropriate visual material on the opened-up inside sheet

Diagram 5–1.

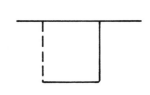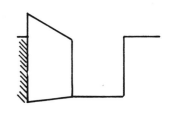

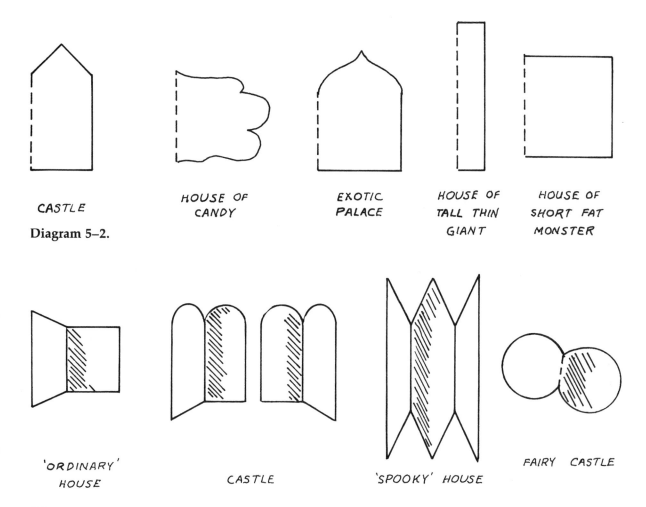

CASTLE

HOUSE OF
CANDY

EXOTIC
PALACE

HOUSE OF
TALL THIN
GIANT

HOUSE OF
SHORT FAT
MONSTER

Diagram 5–2.

'ORDINARY'
HOUSE

CASTLE

'SPOOKY' HOUSE

FAIRY CASTLE

Diagram 5–3.

(see Diagram 5–4). To draw directly through the doorway can lead to unwanted crayon and pen markings on the front page.

Just as the contour triggers a visualizing inventiveness in story making, so engineered openings redirect the story-making technologist into a new realm of thinking. Opening a door is to imply, metaphorically at least, that one must go through it. This journey takes the thinking eye into—or out of—a new episode that would not otherwise be available to the imagination. When we actually see what is on

Diagram 5–4.

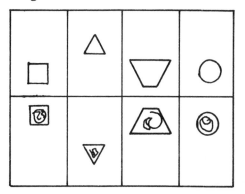

the other side, whether it is a field or a cellar, the necessity to construct thematic artwork elicits a narrational response. Through the cellar door we see . . . ? And it is that speculation that introduces new possibilities, characters or situation analysis to the child. Once children have internalized the opening concept they invent situations to use it. The familiar cry of "Can I have a door here, please?" signifies a self-motivated level of involvement. It is so easy for the engineered opening to be a novelty feature and little else. It is essential that its full potential is used in developmental concept formation. A carefully constructed plot may need reworking because a door suggests a new direction for it. Seeing stolen gold inside a box can help revitalize an ailing narrative.

Improvisory Techniques

Doors and windows can operate on flat-topped concertina books or be used in conjunction with contours. Cut some doors/

Diagram 5–5.

windows, as in Diagram 5–5, and discuss with the class what kind of container, object, or building the openings suggest. Can a story be woven between them?

Investigating the Genre

There is a great deal of story-making imagery that can be uniquely stimulated by the engineered-door technique. Apart from the meaning implicit in the type of door or window, its placing presents another line if inquiry. Where and how it is engineered on the page is crucial to the imagery it releases into the imagination (see Diagram 5–6).

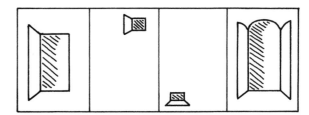

Diagram 5–6.

1.   A centrally placed door implies a front door entrance.
2.   A small door at the top of the page suggests a trap door in the ceiling or high prison cell window.
3.   Conversely, a small door at the bottom of the page suggests a trap door leading down into a cellar.
4.   A larger opening suggests a door at the bottom of a house . . . or top.

Just as one can develop thematic ideas by improvising contour shapes, so narratives can be developed by investigating either a blank "openings" book or a series of chalkboard drawings.

This is a transcript of an "openings" game with a class of eight-year-olds (see Diagram 5–7).

Miranda the Mermaid **Student (22 x 15 cm; 9 x 6 in). This eye-catching visual aid was designed to stimulate children into making a story book using this approach.**

Q.   What kind of door is the first one?
A.   A door into a haunted house, a secret door in a castle, a car door.
Q.   Let's say a haunted house. If we go through the door, what's inside? What does the second door suggest?
A.   A secret trapdoor.
Q.   And where does it lead?
A.   Into a room full of gold, ghosts . . . it's pitch black.
Q.   OK, so it's pitch black inside and we have to feel around in the dark. And then we feel something. What is it—the shape on page 3?

Diagram 5–7.

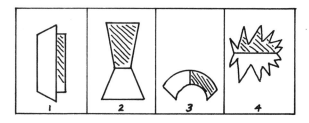

A.   A banana, bundle of money, a box.
Q.   So you've decided on a bundle of money. So how does this lead us to the final shape?
A.   It looks like lightning, an explosion, a crown, a splash, ghosts.
Q.   So how do we connect money with these things?
A.   In the dark you fall into a well (splash!) and lose your money. Ghosts suddenly appear and you run out of the house leaving the money behind.

Developmentally, one can extend the openings to more abstract shapes or engineer more than one to the page. Diagram 5–8 is one example of multiple openings on each page.

• *Page 1:*   It's a hot sunny day in Africa (door in house, sun in sky).
• *Page 2:*   We go inside. An Egyptian mummy leans against the wall, and through the window we can see the desert.

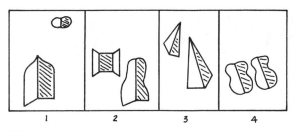

Diagram 5–8.

• *Page 3:* We go on a journey and eventually arrive at the pyramids.
• *Page 4:* Two more mummies are discovered; they come to life.

One of the surprising things about openings is how different the opened form can be to the closed one. What looks like a letter B before opening becomes the numeral 8 or a butterfly after opening (see Diagram 5–9). This mirror image can change the way the image is reconceived. Likewise, where you put

Diagram 5–9.

Diagram 5–10.

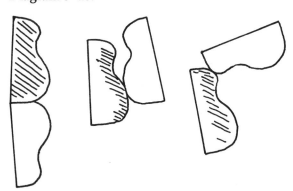

the hinge affects the overall appearance of the form and the subsequent image it makes in the open state (see Diagram 5–10).

In addition to hinged openings, hole shapes can produce another species of forms. To illustrate this genre I have selected just a few of the many inventive and original investigations by children I have been fortunate enough to see.

Alexandra's book (Figure 5–1) is one of the largest concertina books I have come across while visiting schools. It is made of stout card, so supports well the large engineered openings of the four front panels. Inside the openings are heavy fabric collages, which would have been impossible in a book of light- or medium-weight paper.

Alexandra saw engineered books made by older children and wanted to make one herself. The engineering was done by the teacher one page at a time at the direction of the child. Page 1 ("I saw a queen on my way home.") was written on lines made for her and preceded by collage artwork. Page 2 artwork is a self-portrait ("I thought I would go up to her and speak to her"). The teacher explained how at this point she asked Alexandra, "And what did she say to you?" And so page 3 is a dialogue: "Hello, what's your name?" "My name is Alexandra Dunn." Page 4 sees them going off to the collaged castle: "We went to a castle and played with the princess." On the unengineered reverse side of the book the artwork changes to mixed media—paper cupcake liners, pipe cleaners, plastic netting. Alexandra wanted new materials for this side of the book, so the waste fabric collection was raided for suitable material. Page 5 sees the author and princess playing games: "We played dominoes and laughed." On page 6 the pastry cases have inspired a tea party: "We had our tea it was a ll cakes yummy." The last page completes the cyclical journey: "Then she waved her magic wand and I was home in bed."

Figure 5–1. *An Adventure with a Princess* Alexandra (5) (20 x 20 cm; 12 x 8 in).

Without this large-format book the experimental collage illustrations would not have been possible, and therefore the story that evolved from them would not have been forthcoming either. Every part of this book-assembling process has influenced every other part. A gradual step-by-step approach by the teacher, easing the child into the multifarious book concept, has produced this above-average, sequentially developed narrative.

Mark, a special needs pupil, was motivated to write by the simple technique of a lifted flap on the cover of a contour book made by a student attached to the school (see Figure 5–2). The cutout eye shape fascinated Mark, and in a few seconds he had produced the idea of a lost eyeball. A student teacher working with him said, "This book sparked off a desire in him to write which was unprecedented."

Lyndsey conceived of hinged doors as text-only areas (see photo). Thus one reads the narrative sequence first then lifts the page to see the accompanying illustration. Lyndsey took ownership of her book already cut and folded by the teacher. It is a landscape

orientation made by cutting a large sheet of drawing paper in half on the landscape horizontal and then folding down again in the conventional concertina way. Lyndsey designed the whole book herself without assistance and made it entirely at home. She is one of a small group of children who have

Figure 5–2. *The Lost Eye* **Mark (10) (23 x 15 cm; 9 x 6 in).**

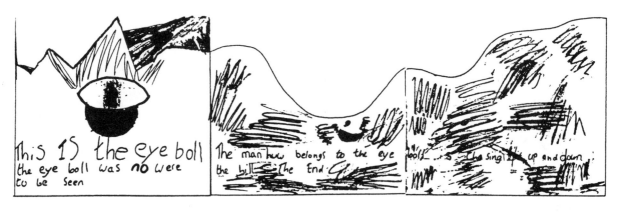

The Passage Way **Lyndsey (8) (16 x 11 cm; 6 x 4 in).**

been formed into a book art group because they like making them so much. They are drawn from two different classes of the same age range and meet about once a month to share story ideas and book-constructing methods they've experimented with, but most especially to show the book they've made since the last meeting. They lay in front of them all the books they've published over the year, which are kept in personalized folders. Self-criticism is encouraged. To boost their confidence they are made to feel that they have achieved an impressive oeuvre: that the better they become at publishing new, high-quality titles the more they must know about making and improving books.

Project books

Project books grow out of pupils identifying a special interest which is then researched, drafted, and organized into a basic book structure. "All About Ghana" is from a class project with ten-year-olds. The pupils practiced the folding sequence on waste paper, and when they perfected the folded, four-page concertina they graduated to large-format drawing paper and did the same. As was discussed earlier, there are two ways of proceeding from here: (1) explore a theme and select forms appropriate to engineering; (2) let engineering experiments suggest a theme. The teacher combined both: brain-storming and thematic starting points, local history, current events, and ecology; and discussing what objects would be relevant to paper engineering and then improvising hinged forms and brainstorming themes from them. The teacher's instructions were to design a book of either four or eight pages with hinged openings on all or most front pages.

In her book, Jemima celebrates her African roots. She describes Ghana, the part of it she comes from, her family, the Ghanain

life-style, naming customs, the village infrastructure, and education. She concludes her autobiographical sketch with a Ghanain coin and postcard fastened into the final two pages. The written structure was organized within the eight pages. After drafting, this was transferred to the concertina book, leaving spaces for engineered artwork. The back four pages lack the finish and design awareness of the front four, but nevertheless it is an engaging piece of work and the sense of achievement that has been generated by producing it is immeasurable.

> When I was on holiday there (Ghana) I knew that when I came home I would want to be able to say something about it all. . . . Making a book like this one just seems so right somehow. . . . It wouldn't be the same just put in a folder . . . I don't think I could ever write just in an ordinary book again. . . .

Jessica's book deals with pilgrimage, an aspect of world religions studied by her class. Some parts of the book were copied off the chalkboard and then rewritten in the children's own words, and other parts were researched from books and schools' TV programs on the subject. There was also an opportunity for personal reflections. The students produced several different concertina book forms, including a standard four-fold and a more unusual three-fold one. The folding process was a teacher/pupil and pupil/pupil collaborative effort. Once the paper was folded, the authors planned the whole book before commencing their research. In Jessica's book the eight pages have been divided into the great religions, and where insufficient space was available, extra pages have been grafted in.

• The title-page door lifts to reveal an introduction to the concept of pilgrimage.
• Pages 1 and 2 describe and illustrate a "special journey" the author has undertaken in her lifetime.

All About Ghana Jemima (10) (21 x 15 cm; 8 x 6 in).

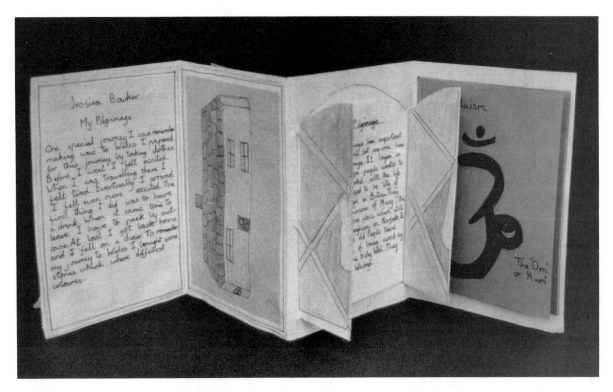

The Meaning of Pilgrimage **Jessica (8) (21 x 15 cm; 8 x 6 in).**

• Page 3 describes pilgrimage in a Christian context; stained glass windows open to text.
• Page 4 introduces Hindu pilgrimage. This a folded sheet, glued in on one side and opening as a leaflet.
• Page 5 is, in effect, the back page, and the artwork symbolizes the crescent and star of Islam.
• Page 6 describes the Muslim's pilgrimage.
• Finally, page 7 celebrates Judaism in an attached leaflet form like that for page 4.

The projects were completed over several weeks.

David's cover (Figure 5-3) is also a carefully balanced planning of words and symbols. Both examples show the very high standard of design achievable by relatively young children when task-oriented programs of study are processed through the book arts.

Figure 5–3. *My Book About Pilgrimages* **(cover) David (8) (15 x 14 cm; 6 x 5 in).**

Figure 5–4 and Figure 5–5. Two pages from *Pilgrimage* (doors open and closed) Gillian (9) (15 x 14 cm; 6 x 5 in).

chapter 6

The Extended Concertina

From the concertina engineered with doors and windows, there is one other dimension—a third dimension—that cannot be omitted from this survey of the concertina book genre. The vast domain of the three-dimensional pop-up book excites and stimulates children of all ages. I have attempted to identify the basic language of the 3-D book genre elsewhere (Johnson, 1992). Here it is explored in one of its simplest manifestations—that of 90 degree angled engineering. As will be seen, it is capable of reorientating the whole concept of processing ideas through the books arts.

Books in the Nursery

To begin with, I want to show the influence of the 3-D book on four-year-old children and its potential to advance their cognitive development. To do this I am illustrating two kinds of books—the hinged-door type and the 180 degree pop-up engineered book. The hinged-door approach, already discussed, will be presented in another form, but the developmental pop-up book will not be discussed in analytical engineering terms. The reason for this is that there just isn't space to define this technology within the context of an innovative curriculum framework.

There is a tendency to assume that young children are incapable of sequencing or, indeed, recalling personal events or experiences other than those in their immediate experience; that what happened last week or last month is a hazy, almost indefinable and certainly irretrievable territory of the child's cognition. The work of children at Reddish Vale Nursery in Stockport brings that notion into question, as the children's books illustrated here will show. Margaret, one of the teachers at the nursery, came to a children's book art course I organized for Stockport teachers. Among the book forms explored was the concertina.

When Margaret showed her three- and four-year-olds what she had made, they not surprisingly wanted to make books like them. So she folded large sheets of drawing paper in half on the horizontal format and then folded this strip down to four concertina folds. Margaret then discussed with her group of enthusiastic children what they wanted to "say" in their books. All the ideas were autobiographical in context and related to experiences that, for various reasons, had been important to them. Through personal dialogue they were encouraged to visualize the folds as "episodes," like "real" books. The title page was designated as the last fold on the rear of the book, creating seven pages for sequencing.

Pupils were asked to describe the first episode of their chosen experience and to say as much about it as possible. This provided a brainstormed reconstruction from which the child could then draw visual images, using felt pens and crayons and, where appropriate, symbols of writing. If doors or windows were required, Margaret engineered them into the page.

Caution was required in checking that openings did not coincide. For example, page two backs onto page seven. No one was allowed to progress to page two until Margaret considered that the conceptual framework of page one had been fully realized. When the stage of recall had been explored to its full potential, pupils were permitted to draw the results on page two. This process continued through the folds, but over several days. It was as if the ability to concentrate on the task of developmental recall could only be handled in discrete units, a day (or a gap of several days) apart. Completing the book could therefore take a week or more. What is interesting is that however long the period between recalling, "Imagising" sessions, the chosen experiences did not seem to fade.

Two examples of children's work are illustrated here. First is Catherine's (4 years 2 months) account of her holiday (see Figure 6–1). These flashbacks into the child's history are illuminating in the accuracy and vividness of the experience communicated. The garden is richer in definition than the schematic flowers on a baseline so typical of early

symbolic imagery. It is an aerial view recording flowers, trees, and swing in topographical detail.

Each page (or double page) is an independent yet related unit, and through discussion with the teacher an indivisible meaning has been given to them. Pages 1, 2, 5, 6, 7 are single sequences, but pages 3 and 4 are conceived as one page. It is inconceivable that six progressive stages of an event in the life of one so young could have been tabulated so cohesively without the concrete structure of the book form. The folds of the book symbolize a change or modification of sequential experience. They act as a line on which to hang ideas, boxes in which concepts are stored and reviewed where necessary.

- *Page 1:* This shows Catherine and Mummy in their house looking out through the engineered door.
- *Page 2:* Leading from the house is the road that takes them all the way to Kent where they are going on holiday. The car they are travelling in is drawn in two places en route. The long distance is symbolized by the sheer complexity of the map.
- *Page 3/4:* On the way they stop at a service station. Engineered doors show both passengers alighting from the car.
- *Page 5:* Finally they reach their destination, the house in Kent.
- *Page 6:* Catherine describes the s-shaped garden of the house in graphic detail. There are trees and flowers around the edge of the lawn, and at the far end there is a swing where Catherine played every day.
- *Page 7:* At the back of the house is a room where Mummy did the washing. Behind the engineered door is drawn a washing machine and a clothesline.
- *Page 8:* Title page.

A flat sheet of paper, although having the potential to convey complex transitions

Figure 6–1. *My Holiday* **Catherine (4) (21 x 16 cm; 8 x 6 in).**

of time, as in the strip-cartoon strategy, or indeed conventional writing itself, is beyond the symbol-making resources of the essentially preliterate child. Consequently, the four-fold concertina is within the child's grasp, and the challenge is to make those folded pages one's own. The teacher's role is to ease the sequencing out of the book artist. However, the four-fold concertina has its limitations. If the exercise book is too big and daunting, the personal handmade book may be too small. Catherine's story terminated with the scullery at the back of the house because that was the last page. Would she have continued if more pages had been available? Could her holiday diary develop into recorded images of other aspects of her holiday—places visited, surprises, special treats? We have no way of knowing.

Inevitably, the next stage of this exploration into the pupil's thinking and image-making was to produce books with more pages. I made a number of six-fold concertina books, facilitating twelve possible

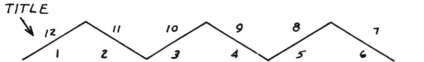

TITLE

Diagram 6–1.

sequences. I left these with Margaret and returned to the nursery a few weeks later to see the results. To my pleasure there was a collection of completed twelve-page books by the children. But these had developed in other ways as well, for they contained pop-ups. Margaret had been introduced to the magical world of pop-up engineering in the book art course referred to earlier. The children wanted to make them too, and so they appeared throughout the books, on hinged pages 1/2, 3/4, 5/6, 8/9, and 10/11, although not all the pages were designed in this way (see Diagram 6–1).

The Twelve-Page Pattern

Margaret showed pupils how to make the pop-up forms from their drawn objects, but the engineering task was beyond their conception. The book I have chosen to illustrate this form is by Sian (4 years 2 months). The extra folds have clearly enabled Sian to extend recorded autobiographical episodes beyond those possible in a smaller book.

• *Title Page:*   Sian and Mummy going to school.
• *Pages 1/2:*   Sian, Jade (sister), and Mummy arriving at school. The lights are on and Mummy is wearing her long black coat.
• *Pages 3/4:*   Sian went to play on the verandah. There was clay on the round table, yellow toys in the sand, and milk bottles in the water play.

• *Page 5:*   Jade came in the afternoon. If you lift the flap you can see the bones inside her.
• *Page 6:*   They went home, up the steps to the house.
• *Page 7:*   Mummy made Sian a lovely bedtime drink. It was hot and there was steam on the top.
• *Pages 8/9:*   Sian lying in bed under her striped duvet cover. Mummy (still in her long black coat) tucks her up.
• *Pages 10/11:*   Sian goes to the nursery the next morning and finds that the chicks have hatched.

Catherine's book specifies events in sequence, but the chronology is less specific than Sian's, who identifies the division of the day into:

1. early morning, going to school,
2. morning activities,
3. sister joining her in the afternoon,
4. going home later in the afternoon,
5. evening drink,
6. going to bed, and
7. going to school the next morning.

Without the book form all this processed thought would have been impossible. Another important observation is the nature of what has been recalled, particularly the minutiae of experience (e.g., the accuracy of the nursery play activities, Mummy's long black coat, the steam rising from the hot drink). Through these visual images we witness the child's cognition and enter into the conceptualization of remembered experiences, which may possibly even surpass our own!

My Book **Sian (4) (21 x 16 cm; 8 x 6 in).**

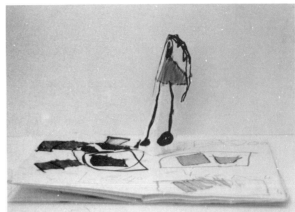

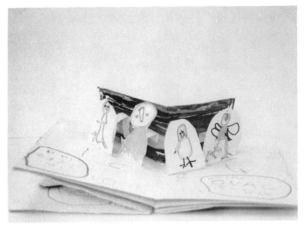

The credit of course goes to Margaret, whose determination to introduce her pupils to the book arts produced such impressive evidence for learning potential in the nursery. I had discussed with her whether or not it would be appropriate to stretch the book concept even further, to sixteen or twenty pages, or even more. Perhaps having children maintain a visual journal of not just one day's experience but two, three, indeed a whole week, is a stage more appropriate to older pupils. Maybe it is just a matter of time, that most elusive of influences on our evolution, for Margaret's children to demand more pages in order to continue or complete a biographical episode from their lives.

One thing is certain: If children of four years of age can sequence in twelve or more stages then we are underestimating what older children can achieve. What kind of books will Catherine and Sian be writing at six or eight? If teachers are unaware of the power of the book form to concretize and process thought, to give visual symbolism to stored experience, and to enthuse young children into wanting to make one, then such development will not be forthcoming.

The 90 Degree Pop-up Engineered Book

The easiest way to understand this technique is to simulate the following (see Diagram 6–2):

1. Fold duplicating paper in half; cut two parallel lines, (not more than halfway across the page) across fold through both sheets.
2. Crease central area towards you.
3. Fold back again.
4. Open folded sheet to inside; push central panel inward to make pop-up form.

For a pop-up to pop up it must cross a fold. Thus on the four-fold concertina three pop-ups are possible: two on the front and one on the back (see Diagram 6–3). What is particularly exciting is to explore the range of possible 3-D forms. The dual approach of all the other engineering activities already discussed apply here: either you explore what kind of engineering is required to make the form you want or you improvise forms and brainstorm images/sequences/developments to give meaning to them. Of the many hundreds of basic pop-up techniques, one is illustrated in four variations (see Diagram 6–4).

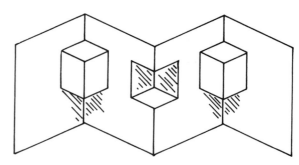

Diagram 6–3.

Diagram 6–2.

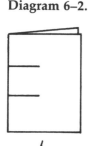

1

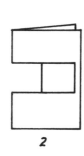

2

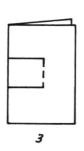

3

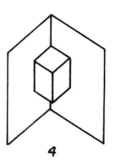

4

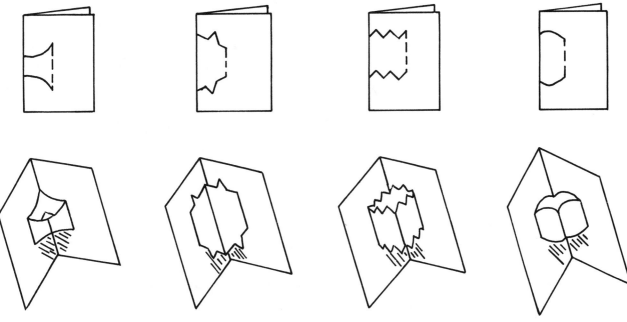

Diagram 6–4.

When an angled hinge supports an engineered section, the resulting form is quite different from the vertical orientation (see Diagram 6–5).

1. Cut rainbow-type section and hinge on the diagonal; do not engineer too low on the page or the form will protrude beneath the page.
2. Fold down form
3. Push form through to inside of page as before.

The 3-D book genre introduces new visualizing concepts about narrative development. To start with, the fold between pages, a no-go area in the conventional concertina, has an important role to play. The fold itself now sprouts a form of its own so that the fold, far from being a transitional point, is an active participant in and on the book's panorama (see Diagram 6–6). Of course one loses part of the page by the pop-up itself, but this is more than compensated for by this new sculptural addition. In developmental terms, the book journey now becomes another kind of experience over, under, and *through* space. The positioning of the pop-up form is another indicator of symbolic meaning. Placed high on the page it is a spaceship; placed low, a house, factory, or shop; placed halfway up

Diagram 6–5.

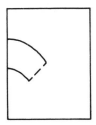
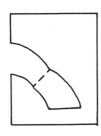
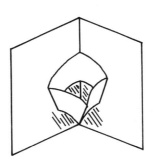

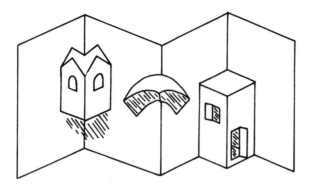

Diagram 6–6.

pop-ups can all be engineered with scissors so children with scissor-cutting skills can explore the genre relatively unaided. The pop-up form is just another concertina shape so that doors and windows can be engineered into them as in all other concertina books.

From experimenting with basic forms it will soon be discovered that more than one pop-up can be engineered on a fold, thus creating top, middle, and bottom images. (It is also possible to design asymmetrically, which established another dimension of picture book thinking.)

The engineering shown so far has been executed on single sheets. When paper is folded on the landscape horizontal and that becomes the engineering base, another dimension of visualization is encountered (see Diagram 6–8).

the page it becomes a tree house. In fact, the spatial element is more complex than that because there are different concepts one can apply to the page, depending on the way one looks at it. The box-like basic form lends itself to all structures loosely box-like—buildings, presents, cupboards, trains; and the diagonally formed pop-up suggests mouths, beaks, bridges (see Diagram 6–7). Ninety degree

1.   Fold a four-fold concertina. Sketch in pop-up forms to first two folds and in the central fold on the reverse side.

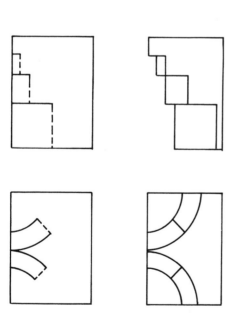

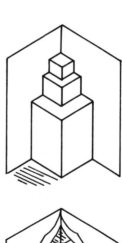

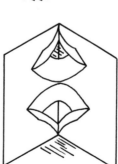

Diagram 6–7.

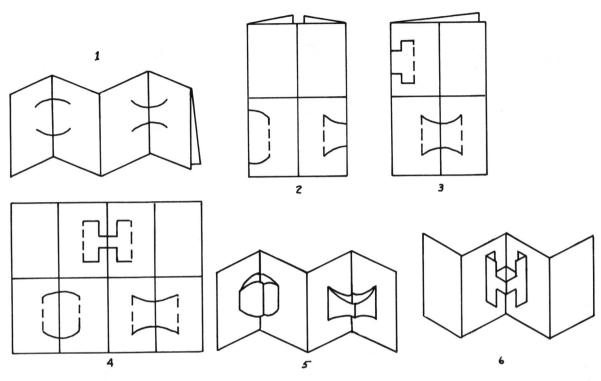

Diagram 6–8.

2. Open up to full sheet and fold first and last folds backward. Engineer forms on bottom panels through double thickness.

3. Open up full sheet and fold on central vertical fold. Engineer form as before but in top panel.

4. Open up full sheet.

5/6. Fold on landscape horizontal. Concertina folds. Raise pop-ups—two on the front panels and one on the back.

The advantage of doubling the paper is that the book artist can pictorialize the interior of houses and shops, create backgrounds to bridges, and add new scenic devices. To do this, the outline of the pop-up form should be sketched through to the back panel, the whole page opened, and the artwork drawn onto the appropriate space. It might seem obvious to make this point, but I have often seen children trying to draw the interior of a form *through* the form itself!

One or Both Sides Programming

The engineering concept can be processed on one or both sides of the concertina book. It is possible to combine any technique with any other; the only difficulty comes when openings or pop-ups must be designed not to coincide with one another. Some children I have work with have had to rewrite part of a story because in its original form it would have been impossible to engineer spatially. In such circumstances problem solving meets its finest hour!

Alex's book, "Mick on Mars," was precut but folded in half. The top contour was of

Mick on Mars **Alex (10) (23 x 11 cm; 9 x 4 in).**

the mirror-image kind already described (see Diagram 6–9). It was suggested to Alex that he decide on the interpretation of the first contour shape and then develop a plot from that. He shared the structuring of his narrative with a partner and between them they produced:

1. Lightening. Mick and his friend were playing football
2. Mick grasps the ball and is carried into space.

pop-up represents football, ground

3. He arrives on Mars and joins the football team.
4. He is carried back to earth the same way as he came.

pop-up of Mars City scarf

Diagram 6–9.

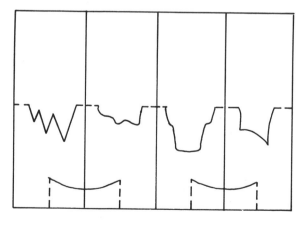

The drafted story was written in the center of the four pages. Alex then completed the drawings above and below the text.

The instructions were that he was to design a 3-D picture book to be published for children. The written and visual ideas had to be clearly and simply expressed. Published and children's self-made books in the genre were used as visual aids.

Sarah and Fran's book was made on the large-format paper, enabling two authors to work on it simultaneously. The mirror-image contours and three pop-up forms were precut (fifteen in all, one for each pair of children in the class; see Diagram 6–10).

Image identity games were played, similar to the ones described beginning on

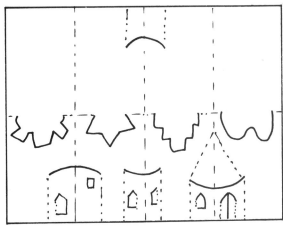

THE MUSICAL ADVENTURE CUTTING DIAGRAM

Diagram 6–10.

The Musical Adventure **by Sarah (11) and Fran (11) (35 x 16 cm; 14 x 16 in).**

page 61 (e.g., "How many different ideas can we have for this shape?"). The task was for the coauthors to visualize a narrative through the engineering sequence of the four pages. The choice was then to either illustrate the mirror-image contours or start the drafting process. Most selected the artwork process, delaying the writing task for as long as possible!

In Sarah and Fran's book, one worked on the artwork for page one contour (the sun), the other on page two contour (a star); while working they talked about what the story would be. Sarah, a musician, decided that the pop-ups would be (1) a boy's house, (2) a violin shop, and the third was as yet undecided. Next they drew in the pop-up house, the boy inside (Sarah), the violin shop (Sarah, Fran), and the shop interior in page two contour (Fran). The story, about a boy—Amadeus—who breaks a violin in a violin shop and then runs into a church to hide, was drafted (first part Fran, second part Sarah) and then written into the spaces at the bottom of the pages. Deciding the end of the story in relation to the contour's shape was a joint effort and worked on accordingly; by this stage they were completely at ease with one another, drawing in the same space simultaneously! The whole task was completed in three hours.

The weakness of this book is that the narrative does not sequence very effectively.

But the aim of this session was to develop sophisticated co-authorship skills so that children like Sarah and Fran will have the knowledge and confidence to conceive and construct a three-dimensional picture book entirely of their own design in the future.

The Extra-Extended Concertina

To complete this appraisal of the ever-expanding concertina I turn to the uses of pockets and containers, and the *ad infinitum* book continuum.

In this first book the objective was two-fold: to engage pupils in groups of six in a collaborative, information-gathering, assimilating, and communicating task; and to realize their efforts in a concertina book form. They had already experienced the concertina in many different forms, so this was a logical progression.

Describing the Book Form

I felt it would be more practical and save a lot of wasted time later, if, before topics were discussed, they had rooted into their imaginations how their investigations would be processed and delivered. In front of them was a complete book comprising three attached four-fold concertina sections with a range of pockets, pop-ups, "tramlines,"

Diagram 6–11.

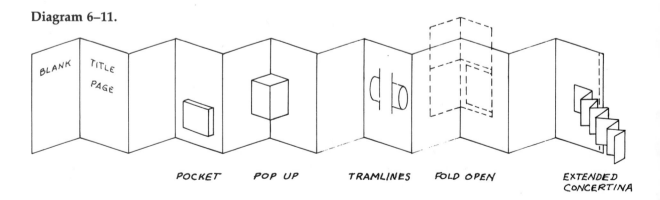

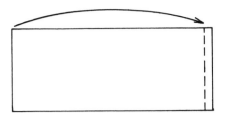 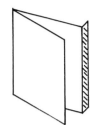 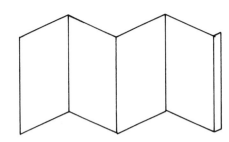

Diagram 6–12.

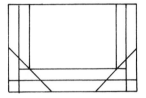 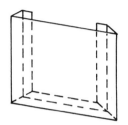

Diagram 6–13.

and other paper gadgets (see Diagram 6–11). In a pile were a set of about twenty, four-fold sections, and the class was shown how these could be added on to one another, right around the world if need be (see Diagram 6–12). The first page of the first section would be left blank as this would eventually be attached to the book's cover. The next page would be the title page, but from there on the rest of the book was open to speculation. The various holding devices on the pages were described as follows:

• *The pocket*: This was to contain folded objects (folders, booklets, maps that were too large or precious to be glued into the book or slotted in (see Diagram 6–13).
• *The pop-up*: This technique provided either a visually manifested concept or a support for applied material.
• *Tramlines*: This is a very simple technique for holding thin objects, like folded sheets of paper or letters, requiring only two lines to be cut on the page (see Diagram 6–14).

• *Folded and glued*: A way of presenting work that is too large for the concertina format (drawings, posters) is to fold it down to a smaller size and then glue the rear side of the bottom right side panel to the book page.
• *Concertina within a concertina*: This is a way to elongate the book without adding extra pages to the basic structure. A smaller concertina is fastened down to the book's page and held into place by a strip.

The book cover was not discussed at this stage. Once the form had been grasped it was time to turn to the theme.

Diagram 6–14.

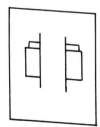 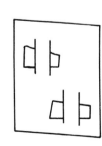 

Work Patterns

The groups were asked to discuss a project theme for their book. Ideas came forth: transport through the ages, famous people, fashion, great artists, mysteries, and the two great World Wars. They were given an introduction to research method ("How can we find out about . . . ?"), using the school library, writing to agencies, designing questionnaires. An editor was elected from each table who would be generally responsible for the organization of the tasks, and each pupil was assigned to at least one double-spread page for their contribution. As tentative ideas became formulated and developmentally consolidated, discussions and report-back sessions assured that the structure and content of the individual contributions related to a collective policy. At strategic points technical inputs were introduced. For example: When is it best to write about something, and when to draw? Should magazine articles be included or should it be all firsthand material?

Rough drafts were done on paper approximately the size of the book page so that its relationship to the finished copy could be gauged. One of the dangers of group project work is that those who have good basic skills in writing or drawing tend to concentrate on these areas at the expense of the other. So one of the rules was that every child should work in both communication systems. A great deal of sharing went on between members within groups and between groups. This included showing their illustrations, describing why they were doing them, and inviting questions about them.

As work was completed it fell to the editor to decide, in collaboration with the rest of the team, what went where in the book, how many four-fold sections would be needed, and how it was to be presented. There were three main ways of doing this—pockets,

tramlines, gluing—and how work was assembled was crucial to the total visual impact of the book. It was also agreed that all works should be mounted.

Notes on Mounting Work

Lightly attach work to be mounted to a corner area of mounting paper, leaving about half a centimeter margin (see Diagram 6–15). It is a principle of mounting that the finer the mount, the better the work looks. Line up the other two sides of the mount and, using cutter and steel ruler, cut the mount free.

A second mount can add just that little extra finish to the appearance of a beautiful piece of handwriting or artwork. A fine black mount can add dignity to whatever it surrounds and pastel shades can add variety, especially where double (or treble) mounts are in use.

Explore colored mounts by laying work to be mounted on a range of colors and color combinations (see Diagram 6–16). We cannot divorce the emphasis we place on children's handwriting and presentation from the

Diagram 6–15.

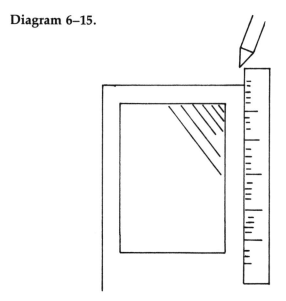

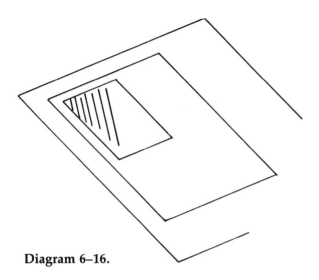

Diagram 6–16.

 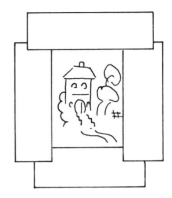

Diagram 6–17.

publishing techniques employed. The way children's work is set off and celebrated through mounting *is* literacy education.

Another technique of mounting applies particularly to artwork. Sometimes it is unnecessary to mount the whole of a piece of artwork. Perhaps there is too much sky, or an empty foreground. Isolate the composition down in size by laying strips of white paper to the four sides of the artwork (see Diagram

6–17). These can be moved in and out until a satisfactory balance is achieved.

The simplest way to make a strong cover for a concertina book is to cut a strong piece of card to slightly larger than the book's dimensions, plus a spine and back cover. The thicker the book's contents, the wider the spine (see Diagram 6–18). These project books may well contain bulky material, so ease pages to the closed position (not too tightly) and estimate the width of spine required. Glue outside pages of the book to the inside of the covers.

Diagram 6–18.

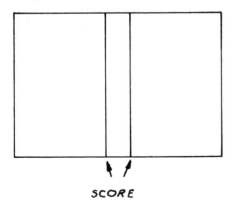

SCORE

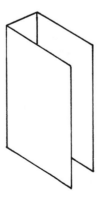

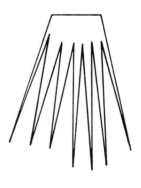

PLAN

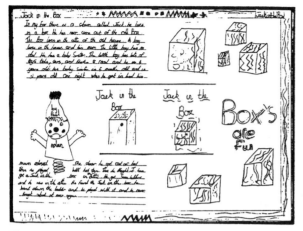

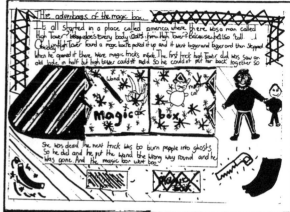

Figure 6–2.

Photographs of whole book presentation.

Concertina Extravaganza

It is possible for the interactive project book to be reduced to individually folded units that are joined together in a chain. In the activity recorded here, two classes of seven-and eight-year-old children combined to make a book of sixty individually produced pages. A simple 90 degree pop-up was projected on each fold and the children given the task of designing a short story to accompany the form's artwork. The process of large-group/

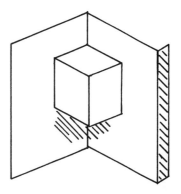

Diagram 6–19.

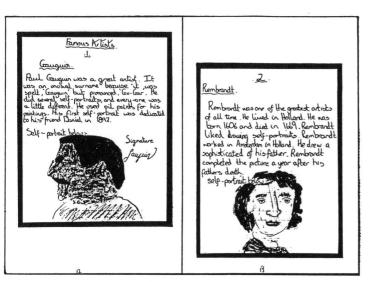

Figures 6–3 through 6–8. Individual pages.

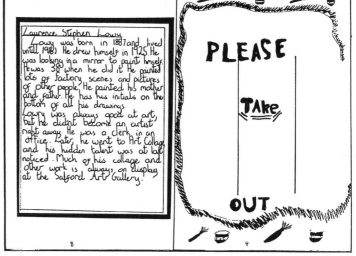

small-group discussion, shared drafting, artwork, design, and final presentation took about three hours, and so the whole sixty-page book was made in half a day!

The units were joined together and bound into the cover only at the front, leaving the book's contents free-standing (see Diagram 6–19). Several different display possibilities suggest themselves, depending on size and design of school classrooms and corridor areas. An approach for small display areas is to show only ten units at a time and for this method to be repeated through the whole book over a three- to six-week period. In this

way every pupil's book is clearly displayed for a four- to five-day period over the span of several weeks.

Comments by children in the class when their book was first displayed:

"I didn't know that you could make a book like this."

"Why don't we make a book made by everyone in the school?"

"I would like to make a book like this which you can just go on adding new bits to whenever you felt like it."

"When do we make the next one?"

part three

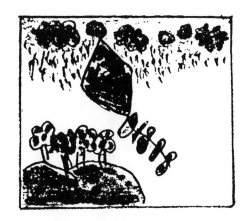

Flight the

Kite by Joanne

chapter 7

The Origami Continuum

The only structural difference between a concertina book and an origami book is a cut across the central panels of the landscape horizontal. Yet that difference produces a spectrum of concepts that are in every way transformative. Although a concertina book can be closed down and the pages turned in the conventional reading fashion, it is without a central, pivotal, spine. As has been discussed, that factor gives the book a freedom and dynamism known to no other book. But there is also a problem with it. The codex style of binding—the central spine—has been with us for over a thousand years, and whether we like it or not it is embedded into our collective psyche. The concertina form, however versatile, will always remain mysteriously alien to our culture and modus operandi. The magic of the origami book is that it is both simple (it comprises eight pages) and looks like a "real book" (it has front and back covers). I say *looks* like a real book, but in fact it has little in common with it. It has no real spine and it has a fixed number of pages. But what it has built into its form is to feel right in the palm of the hand, opening with a clearly defined front cover and closing with a back one. All the origami book variations discussed here have this facility. Diagram 7–1 illustrates the construction of the basic origami.

1. Fold sheet into basic eight folds. Cut through central two landscape panels.
2. Fold on horizontal.
3. Push left and right panels to center, ensuring that the central panels protrude at right angles to create a star. (This will be aided by inserting fingers in the slot.)
4. Fold *any* pages around to make front and back covers and six integral pages.
5. As an alternative to using a cutter, and appropriate where younger children are concerned, use scissors to cut the central panels.

The Origami Concept

The three double-page integral form establishes a new discipline for the young book artist. Thinking must now be organized

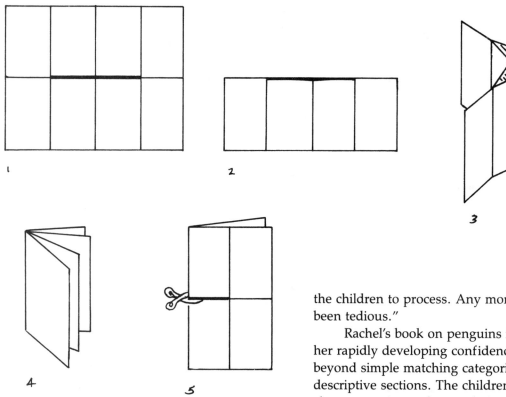

Diagram 7–1.

in three basic parts, and front and back covers are a real design challenge. As the work of children will show, this limitation liberates rather than contracts the imagination. The discussion of the origami book process that follows tries to identify how the form influences cognition and creative action. (To avoid repetition, word and image concepts already discussed have been omitted.)

These two books in Figures 7–1 and 7–2 by Rachel were processed in close proximity to each other and illustrate categorical and descriptive analysis by emergent writers. "Big and Small" books were stimulated by the class teacher discussing the concept and the class brainstorming it. The teacher noted how well the concept fit the structure: "The three double pages were exactly the right length for

the children to process. Any more would have been tedious."

Rachel's book on penguins indicates her rapidly developing confidence to think beyond simple matching categories to six descriptive sections. The children were told about penguins and several visually orientated reference books were available for research. Each page was completed under the teacher's supervision and grouping by pairs ensured a constant sharing of ideas. The teacher said,

> This sharing was essential to the flow and success of the work. They really do help each other think and plan. But the origami book was the most important influence. Rachel would not have developed so fast without it.

"Snakes" (Figure 7–3), from a project on animals, shows just how capable young children are at planning, sequencing, and presenting research-based work. Their classroom contains a comprehensive resource bank of reference books and visual aids.

The children whose work is shown in Figure 7–4 were given the task of describing the experience of a kite in six pages. Both these books and their drafting predecessors were made from photocopying paper. The

Figure 7–1. *Big and Small* **Rachel (6) (15 x 10 cm; 6 x 4 in).**

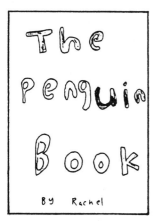

Figure 7–2. *The Penguin Book* Rachel (15 x 10 cm; 6 x 4 in).

Figure 7–3. *Snakes* Gemma (6)
(15 x 10 cm; 6 x 4 in).

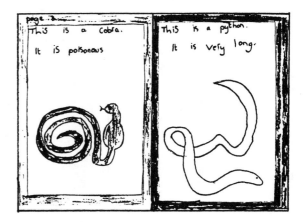

whole book—text and illustrations—were planned in precisely the same size and format as the finished product. It is interesting how many different design approaches have been used to make the cover. The overall playfulness of the theme has been conveyed well. Perhaps Leanne's is the most successful design, demonstrating freedom and restraint. While each book designer has some way to go in providing stylish designs for their books, it is essential that progress is made in an intuitively developmental way.

Figure 7–4. Six covers by six-year-olds from a class story book project, "Flight the Kite."

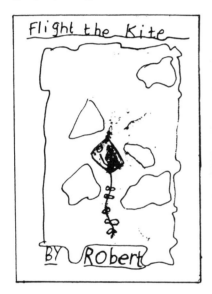

In Figures 7–5 and 7–6 we see more examples of the origami as a model communicator of information or instruction. Road safety is best described in simple, basic rules that must be learned. How these rules are communicated is the task of the designer. The class teacher discussed with the pupils the main tenets of road safety and then they planned their road safety books for an audience of younger children. It would have been a much easier teaching strategy if instructions defining each page had been distributed to the class in the form of worksheets, but such an approach, although producing model examples of clarity, would have been a negative learning experience for those involved. By examining instruction books and analyzing what they say and how they say it, exploring what is best said in words and what in pictures, planning out the contents and covers in an ordered sequence, pupils equip themselves with pragmatic skills of communication that are transferable to a myriad of problem-solving situations.

Figure 7–5. *My Road Safety Book* Michala (8) (13 x 8 cm; 5 x 3 in).

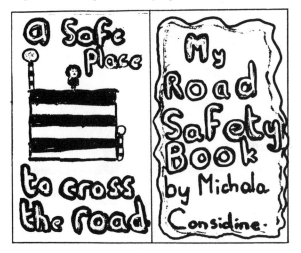

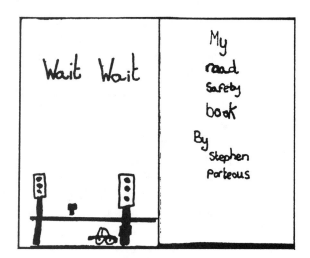

Figure 7–6. *My Road Safety Book* **Stephen (8)** (13 x 8 cm; 5 x 3 in).

This is part of a conversation I had with Stephen about his book:

Q. Stephen, in your book why did you put words at the top and all drawings underneath?
A. The main things you want to say should be easy to read . . . and kept short because young children won't bother to read them if they aren't. . . . They like pictures. . . . They like looking at colorful things so if you can put things in pictures it's better than with words. . . . That's why I put mostly pictures on the page. It's more fun to look at.
Q. Do you think children learn more that way?
A. Yes.

In contrast to Stephen's book, Michala's book relies less on visual communication and more on direct speech— ". . . so what am I going to tell you about is the green cross code." However, page six and the back cover are strongly designed, visually orientated messages.

"The Cat, the Dog, the Rat" is Claire's first book and signifies a landmark in her personal development, for it is the beginning of her motivation to write. The teacher described the delight experienced by the entire class, including Claire, when given a blank origami book. The one-sentence, schematic statements tucked away in the top left corners are not so much written for the desire to make them as the desire to have some material that can make a book. Similarly, the colorwork—

Figure 7–7. *The Cat, the Dog, the Rat* **Claire (7) (11 x 7 cm; 4 x 3 in).**

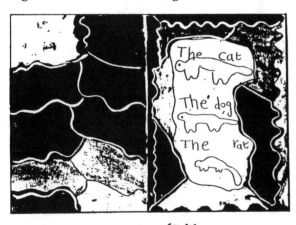

one can barely call them illustrations—are there, one feels, to "fill the pages." It is the pleasure of making a book that has triggered all the marks on paper.

It is hard to believe that Claire's second book (see Figure 7–8) followed directly from the one above. Once Claire had been bitten by the book bug, her desire to make a real book—sequenced story with illustrations—lifted her up to a new plateau of expressive ability. The book, as a concept, had been waiting inside her to be discovered.

In Claire's third successive book (see Figure 7–9) we find her unable to keep up with the flood of ideas that are now pouring out of her. Her skills of writing, and basic grammar, are inadequate to sustain this book-producing energy and the communicating zest it demands. Even the illustrations have been reduced in number to give space for the text.

Figure 7–8. *I went to the Shop* **Claire (11 x 7 cm; 4 x 3 in).**

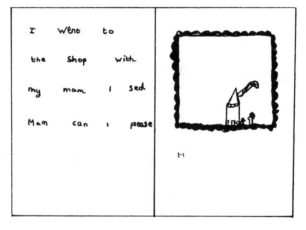

Figure 7–9. *I Sar My Frend* **Claire (11 x 7 cm; 4 x 3 in).**

Basic Origami Variations

Lack of space precludes a comprehensive appraisal of the origami and its variations. The most variable element is the central cut. This can be done in a variety of ways to give a whole new meaning to the form.

To experiment, fold a sheet into four vertical panels and draw a line across the landscape center. Then explore a cutting pattern between the points 'X' (see Diagram 7–2). You can meander the cutter anywhere you like, but avoid going too near the top edge of the sheet. Then fold in the origami fashion. I gave this task to a group of students in training for teaching and they produced over sixty different motifs and designs!

This form also suggests another mode of presentation. The mirror-image central design lends itself to a frontal rather than book-orientated display, as the illustrations that follow show.

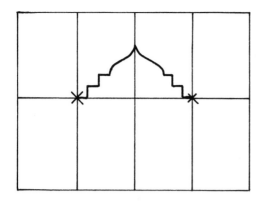

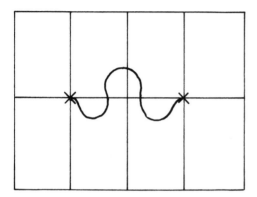

Diagram 7–2.

These last examples demonstrate the organic three-dimensionality of some book forms. In present-day communication, structures like these can be seen at work projecting information for a wide range of commercial and educational uses. Pupils are placed in a learning environment which poses the question: How can this paper best communicate what I want to say?

World Tour **Neil (11) (15 x 10 cm; 6 x 4 in).**

The Filthiest City in Britain
Adam (11)
(15 x 10 cm; 6 x 4 in).

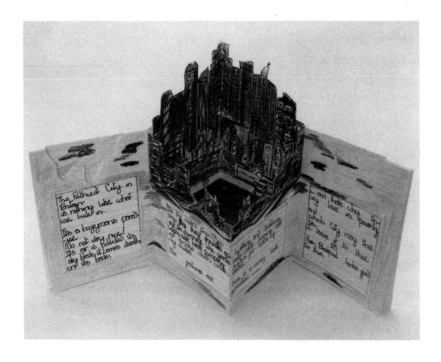

chapter 8

Origami Themes and Variations

In this origami manifestation, the central-cut section is extended by just one panel and this produces a new range of book concepts. Its structure is similar to the concertina and, unlike the basic origami book, is without integral covers. But it has a pivotal hinge, which associates it with the more conventional book structure. It has eight integral pages, although these can be reduced depending on the binding method used.

The Origami Book (Variation 1) with Loose Cover

1. Fold to basic eight divisions (see Diagram 8–1). On landscape horizontal cut through first three pages.
2. Fold down on horizontal. Concertina panels forward.
3. Fold into closed position.

Diagram 8–1.

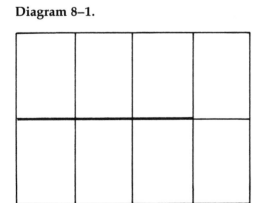

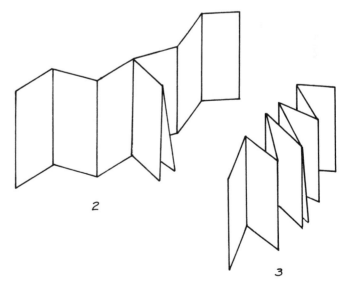

The fold across the top of the middle section tends to cause the pages to spring in an outward direction. The front and back covers, being unattached, tend to spread apart similarly. Therefore, the best way to package this form is inside a detached cover, which also enhances its aesthetic appearance (see Diagram 8–2).

Origami Loose Cover I
1.   Fold same size paper as book on landscape horizontal.
2.   Fold back front flap, leaving 2/3 centimeter between fold and spine.

3.   Repeat step 2 for back flap.
4.   Slot spine into gap in center of book pages.
5.   Fold forward dotted lines (X) flush to book foredge.

A small drop of glue applied to each side of the spinal area will hold the cover firmly into book form.

Origami Loose Cover II
1.   Fold paper same size as book on landscape horizontal (see Diagram 8–3).
2.   Fold over left edge to within 1 centimeter of right edge.

Diagram 8–2.

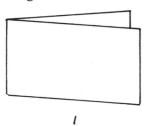

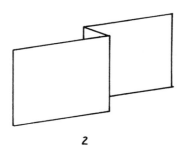

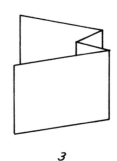

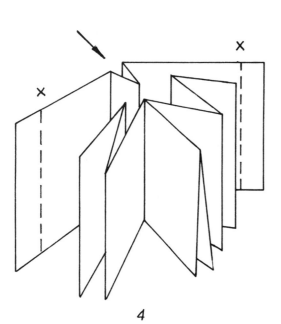

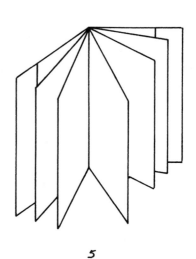

Diagram 8–3.

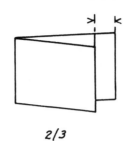

1

2/3

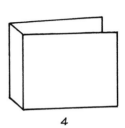

4

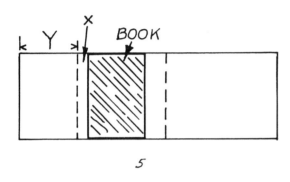

5

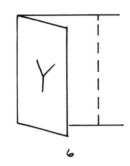

6

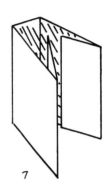

7

3. Repeat step 2, folding right to left.
4. This will automatically make a spine for the cover.
5. Open cover flat. Lay book flush to left side of spine. Mark a point slightly wider than book (X).
6. Fold "Y" forward to make flap.
7. Repeat steps 5 and 6 for right side of cover.
8. Insert outside pages of book into cover slots (B).

This cover holds the book more firmly than cover I, but pages one and eight are lost, as they slip into the cover and are hidden.

To illustrate this particular origami book in a curricular context I turn to one young book artist and his creative evolution in the genre over a short period. I first met Lee when visiting his school in Oldham. He was writing about his holiday in the Lake District of the North of England in an exercise book, and I there and then folded a simple concertina book and asked him if he would like to present

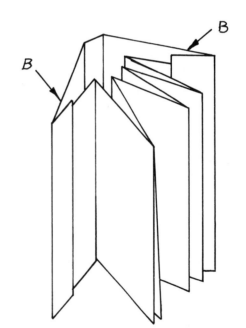

his finished piece of work in book form. I showed him how to lay out his ideas in blocks of writing and illustration. As I left, and much to his surprise, I said I would publish his book on completion.

Figure 8–1 shows the first double page of his first book. There is an intuitive air about it and he describes his experiences with clarity and freshness. "When we got to the house the first thing I did was go to the garden room and set my camera up." I had explained to him that as the book would be photocopied for publication the illustrations would need to be in line, hence the sharpness of his drawings. The book, duly completed, was photocopied in an edition of fifty so that his family, the school, and myself all had copies of his book. About six months later I was in his school again, and it was then that the commissioning strategy occurred to me. Why not encourage

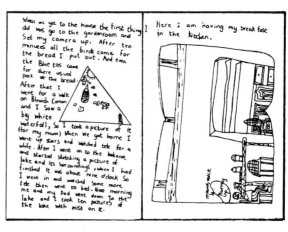

Figure 8–1. *My Holiday at the Lakes* **Lee (7) (10 x 7 cm; 4 x 3 in).**

Figure 8–2. *My Sister* (first version) Lee (8) (15 x 10 cm; 6 x 4 in).

individual children who display a book art flair to make them on a developmental basis, and to use this evolving expertise in stimulating other pupils to do the same?

I asked Lee what he would like his next book to be about, and he said, almost without reflection, "The birth of my sister." I folded down another concertina, twice the size of the standard duplicating proportions, so that the original "camera-ready copy" could be reduced by half for publication, and gave it to him. Some few weeks then passed before Lee's second book was finished.

With this book Lee has made considerable progress from his first book. Words are now written in cursive, the sentence construction and syntax improved, the arrangement of blocks of text and illustration more controlled.

> I'd really like a baby sister. That's what I thought when my mum and dad told me we were going to have a baby. I didn't believe them at first because we're always playing jokes on each other, but when I realized they were telling the truth it was really exciting.

This is a cleanly chiselled beginning with no rough bits. The introductory sentence holds the reader, and the style is consistently maintained until the end: "She's into everything. So what I'd like now—IS A LOCK ON MY DOOR!"

> **Q.** Lee, how did you arrange the book's contents so perfectly?
> **A.** The story I drafted was longer than the book, so as I was writing it I kept leaving out sentences which I thought were less important.

He could have improved the readability of the text by not breaking words; "trou-ble," "broug-ht," and "br-icks" are not only incorrectly hyphenated, they break the eye's natural rhythm of reading the page. He had drawn margins on the pages, which clarified the visual presentation of both word and image forms. But the book lacked the sparkle

of his first one, and one of the reasons for this was the restriction in size. Illustrations have almost been squeezed out. So I made him an origami book with loose cover I, twice the size of the concertina book he had just completed, and asked him if he would like to restructure his book in this new larger format. He liked the idea and thought the way the book was folded was "ace." By using the origami I cover the eight pages of the book's front side and the two cover pages on the reverse combine to make ten processable pages (see Diagram 8–4).

Diagram 8–4.

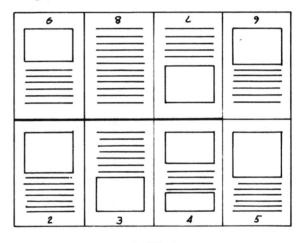

SIDE 1

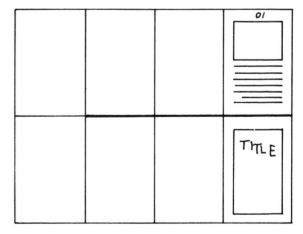

SIDE 2

Figure 8–3. *My Sister* (second version) Lee (8) (21 x 15 cm; 8 x 6 in).

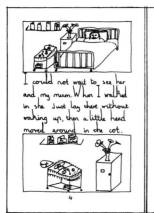

I specified areas for illustration because (1) his account was so pictorial he would have no problem in illustrating it extensively; (2) his visual skills, which had been impeded in his second book, needed space to develop; and (3) he had the potential to construct a book comprising interactive text and illustration. As a preparation for the task of illustrating his text I did a "visual brainstorming" with him, a technique I use extensively with children. I asked him to close his eyes with me and take a visual journey around the maternity ward his mother was in, as this made up the body of his text.

Q. Lee, can you "see" your Mother's bed? Did it have anything by it?
A. Yes, a kind of table.
Q. Did it have doors on it?
A. Yes, with a lock.
Q. What was on the table?
A. A vase of flowers.
Q. Anything near the table?
A. . . . yes, a kind of shelf with cards on it.
Q. Were these congratulations cards?
A. Yes.
Q. Anything near the bed, say lower down?
A. Oh yes, the cot with Elaine (his sister) in it.
Q. Anything on or under the cot?
A. . . . yes, a box of tissues underneath it.

By comparing the illustrations in the two versions, Lee's development is instantly recognizable. The nonspatial self-portrait of the first version is replaced by a greater spatial awareness, stimulated by the visualization in the second. For example, on page four the bed recedes perspectively with the cot in the fore-ground and the congratulation cards in the background. The information contained in his illustrations is not only greater than anything achieved so far, they also contain a second story: the minutely detailed inscriptions in the congratulations cards indicate who they are from, their relationship to Lee's mother, and

the message they have for her. His lines of text are visually harmonious on the page, and he is developing a personal style of handwriting characterized by the exaggerated ascender, which gives a consistently well-designed appearance to his work.

In the tradition of the fine presses, Lee has personalized one or two copies of his published book by hand-coloring the illustrations. This additional dimension to the black-line work evokes even more information than before (e.g., floor tiles and a view through the window).

Figure 8–4. *My Sister II* **Lee (hand colored)**

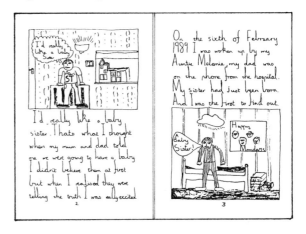

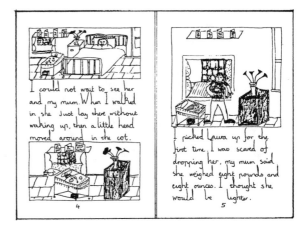

Figure 8–5. *My Holiday at the New Year* **Lee (9) (21 x 15 cm; 8 x 6 in).**

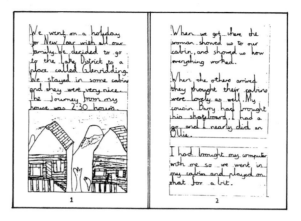

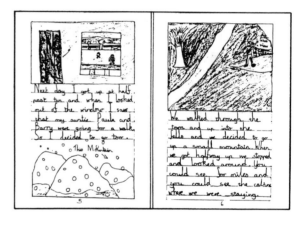

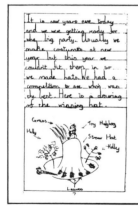

Lee's next commission coincided with another holiday in the Lake District. The quality of the text has moved ahead at a faster rate than that of the illustrations, but there is the same consistency of style produced in his previous book.

> We walked through the town and up into the fells and we decided to go up a small mountain. When we got halfway up we stopped and looked around. You could see for miles . . .

He also has more to record and so lines are drawn closer together for the text. Is he now ready for an even bigger book? Lee said after completing this latest book:

> When I go away on holiday I keep notes about what I've done so that when I get back I can write about it. I wouldn't remember otherwise. I then think about how it might fit into a book. . . . At first it's easy because you just write about things which interest you and you know you can draw about them in the spaces for illustrations. . . . but later, when you realize that there aren't so many pages left you have to think more carefully about what you can put in and leave out. . . . Although I think I find it easier to write than draw, the books wouldn't be the same without pictures. They'd be dull. . . . I know I wouldn't work so hard on writing if it wasn't for putting in a book.

chapter 9

Origami Pop-up Book

This versatile structure lends itself to many transformations and reintroduces the pop-up three-dimensional book genre. I have used it extensively in schools in its more common horizontal manifestations but here it is investigated in its vertical orientation. The origami books previously discussed are made by cutting on the landscape *horizontal*; this book is made by cutting on the landscape *vertical* (see Diagram 9–1).

1. Fold to basic eight panels. Cut the three alternating vertical panels.
2. Drop down the top central panel (X).

3. Fold right half of sheet *over* to the left side.
4. Fold full panels (A) to center, top one forward, back one backward.
5. Drop down top panels in forward and backward direction.
6. Book is now constructed.
7. Number pages 1–8, starting on the first inside page.
8. Open up the book and the pages should be numbered as shown.
9. Drop the top central panel forward again. Through double thickness, cut two parallel lines with cutter or scissors. (They can be curved or straight.)
10. Crease central folds downward.

Diagram 9–1.

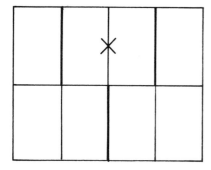 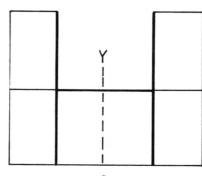 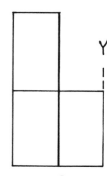

2   3

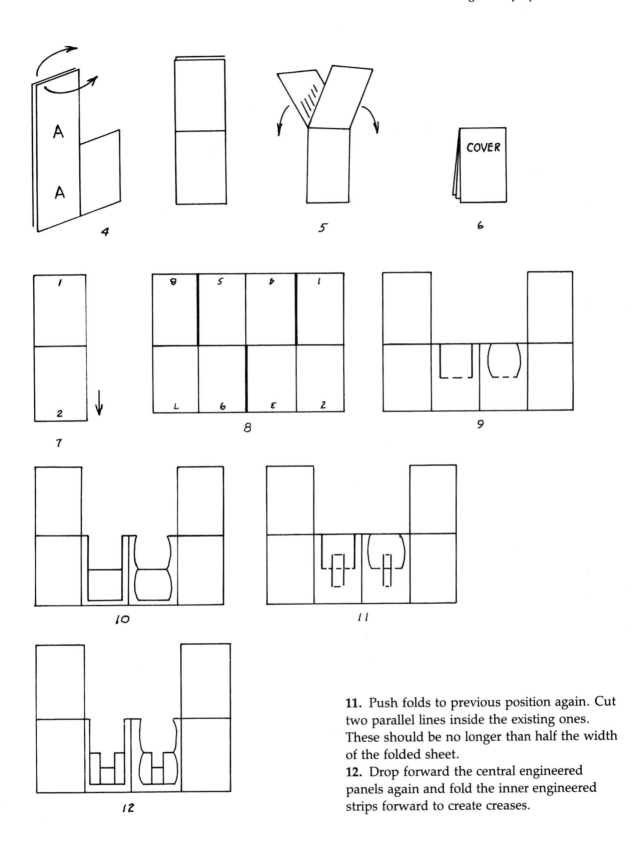

11. Push folds to previous position again. Cut two parallel lines inside the existing ones. These should be no longer than half the width of the folded sheet.

12. Drop forward the central engineered panels again and fold the inner engineered strips forward to create creases.

13. Open up all folds. Cut flaps on the two bottom outside panels, ensuring that points "X" are not higher than points "Y." Fold down large sheet as diagrams 1–6.

14. Open pages 3/4 and 5/6 and push pop-up engineering to 3-D position. Crease open flaps on pages 2 and 7. The book is now ready for REALIZATION!

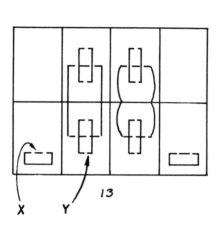

13

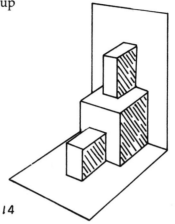

14

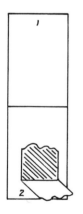

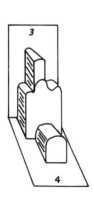

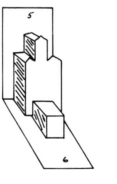

Diagram 9–2.

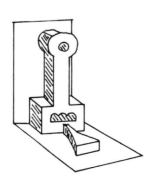

Variations of pop-up forms.

The following is a hypothetical realization of this book form designed by a group of teachers in a book art course:

- *Page 1:* Main character, John, plays in a garden (illustration of garden).
- *Page 2:* John finds a bottle hidden in the bushes (bottle drawn under flap; which represents bush).
- *Pages 3/4:* Hidden inside the bottle is a palace, and when John takes the cork out of the bottle the palace pops out. John cautiously enters palace (pop-up illustration of palace).
- *Pages 5/6:* Inside the palace is another palace, which is even more grand than the first one (pop-up illustration of second palace).
- *Page 7:* John sees a door at the far end of the palace. He opens it and walks through (flap opens to garden).
- *Page 8:* He finds himself back in his garden again, but now there is no bottle and no palaces.

The final task would be to design the front cover and back cover story synopsis, and possibly artwork to back cover.

I was in a school when a teacher said to me, "You must see Phillip's work." His writing was mature even at nine years, and the sketches in the borders of his writing book showed that he was a born illustrator. He was desperately trying to join the two, and the

The Party Phillip (11) (16 x 23 cm; 6 x 9 in).

words too were struggling to be liberated from the writing book that held them like a prison. But he had not yet been introduced to the book concept as a catalyst for his imagination. That was quickly remedied, and that afternoon he took home a ready-made eight-page book. The next week it came back completed—finished at one sitting, or so it seemed, with text and drawings effortlessly extemporized on the pages. A few weeks later he produced "The Party," of which selected pages have been reproduced. It would require several pages to describe the doors he had engineered into the book unaided, and how a secondary story is told through them, and how that is interwoven into the primary story, which itself is complex.

Through the Earth
Phillip (12)
(23 x 16 cm; 9 x 6 in).

Phillip reinvents the book concept whenever he makes one. It consummates his collective skills of communication like nothing else could. Now in high school he no longer makes books, so I continue to commission books from him, which he makes in his spare time. His book "Through the Earth"—in the origami pop-up genre—is one such commission.

- *Page 1:*   Blank
- *Page 2:*   Charlie the crocodile sees a trapdoor in his Auntie's garden. He goes through it (engineered trapdoor, staircase inside).
- *Pages 3/4:*   Charlie comes through another door onto a cliff. A strange bird is in the sky (cliff face on pop-up, swamp at base).
- *Pages 5/6:*   Charlie climbs down the cliff and splashes into the swamp. He sees a door, which he goes through just before the bird jumps on him (the artwork is a repeat of the cliff face on 3/4, but Charlie is now drawn entering the doorway, and the strange bird is halfway down the cliff face).
- *Page 7:*   Artwork of Charlie climbing to the other side of the door; under the flap is a long staircase. Foreground landscape and signpost to Melbourne.
- *Page 8:*   Story describing Charlie arriving in Australia, having travelled through the earth. "There was only one way home, back through the way he came!"

The final example of variations of the origami form is the eight-page origami book. As Diagram 9–3 shows, by cutting an inverted T junction from the central horizontal cut, two extra leaves are created. This converts the basic origami form to an eight-page book.

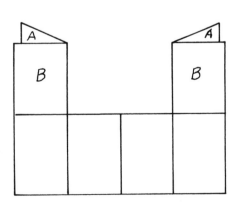

Diagram 9–3.
1. **Fold paper into eight rectangles. Cut as shown.**
2. **Fold flaps A behind flaps B.**
3. **Drop top panels forward.**

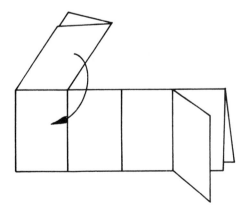

4. Push left and right ends to center.

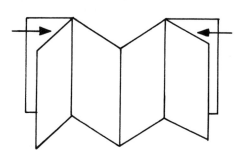

5. Completed book.

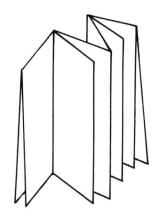

PAGE LAYOUT

SIDE 1

6	8	Ɛ	⅃
BACK COVER			FRONT COVER

SIDE 2

	ⴆ	⅃	
	5	6	

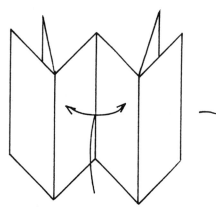

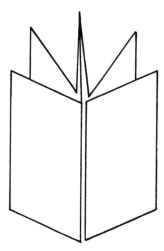

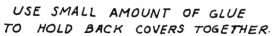

USE SMALL AMOUNT OF GLUE
TO HOLD BACK COVERS TOGETHER.

I have tried to show in Parts Two and Three that the book form is its own process; that implicit in paper technology—the folds, shapes, three-dimensional engineering, and so on—is an invisible yet wholly dynamic process and structure. If you become truly absorbed by the concertina and origami book forms, live within their habitats and listen to them, they will tell you what to do and how to do it. "If you have anything to say, you will know," said Benjamin Britten, "and whatever you have to say will tell you how to say it."

Most of the books included by way of illustration have been produced, in the main, with minimal structuring by teachers. This has not been intentional but because those teachers have been learning about book art simultaneously with their children. Few would see themselves as experts, or even keen amateurs, in art and design; therefore the work they have supervised is pioneering in nature. Teachers have so little to fall back on to assist them. Book art in educational bibliography is almost nil. Teachers have no choice but to rely on these simply constructed books to provide questions and answers. Of course, it does not stop there. We have seen from the statements made by children and their teachers that they learn quickly about the books they are making and how they might be improved and what new challenges indicate the way ahead. Assessing the skills manifested in a finished book requires knowledge of what should, or might, be there. It is also relevant to perceive the readiness of children to comprehend those things and act upon them to bring about change.

part four

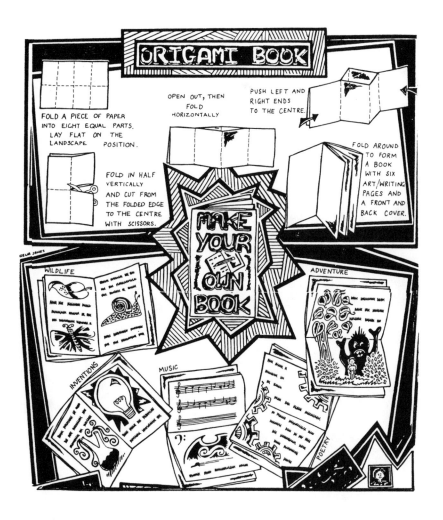

chapter 10

Making Books Work

Paper Technology—Who Does What

Mary, a teacher of eight-year olds distributes junk mail to the class. They start to examine it and look at the brightly colored images, but that is not the aim, at least not on this occasion; for these are for book art. Immediately Mary gives out her folding instructions to the class. Soon all these glossy sheets will be transformed into books.

One question I am often asked by teachers is whether or not I let children make their own books, technologically speaking. It is an impossible question to give a simple answer to because all children are at different executive stages and the layout and design of classrooms varies considerably. And being technologically unskilled does not apply to children only. If teachers are learning new manipulative techniques, then they are at the same stage as the children they teach. Ironically, and I have often found this true in my own case, children may have more advanced craft skills than adults. Having spent almost my entire life working with paper I can now make thirty basic origami books in less than five minutes. The same task could occupy an inexperienced teacher for an hour, or possibly longer. I have taught ten-year-olds who can confidently engineer complex pop-up books using craft

Children's junk mail book experiments.

knives; others of the same age find great difficulty in folding a small piece of paper in half.

Technological skills of folding, cutting, and forming must be taught to children and indeed oneself. Like learning to drive an automobile, one must follow a set procedure. Later, as experience shifts that which is unfamiliar into that which is known, one can deviate from the norm into other patterns of behavior. Working with teachers on practical book art techniques, and starting "from scratch," I use the same ritualistic mantra I use with children:

Now have the sheet of paper in the *landscape* position in front of you . . . *Vertically.* Let's make sure that we all know what vertical is: fold the left side over to the right, make sure that the two sets of corners come together perfectly.

Now crease down the center fold with your other hand—hold the paper steady as you do so. Now lay the folded sheet of paper in front of you in the *landscape* position . . . make sure that your partner has got the sheet round the right way.

Fold it in half again like you did before—on the *vertical.* Remember to hold the corners down with one hand before folding the other. MAKE SURE YOUR CREASES ARE REALLY SHARP.

We need to fold down once more, but there are too many sheets of folded paper here now to make a neat crease so . . . open the fold you have just made and turn your sheet to the *portrait* position—check that your partner has done that.

Now, finally fold the sheet *vertically*, making sure that you line up the corners. Now open up the whole sheet and you have eight folded rectangles.

Doing this over and over can result in the acquisition of quite sophisticated paper engineering skills over a few weeks. The more complex technological techniques exemplified in Parts Two and Three will require newly designed "mantras," but what I find astonishing is the speed with which children accommodate new languages like these. These skills should parallel the developing writing, visual, and design skills of children. Of course, the three rarely go together, which is one of the challenges when cross-curricular learning experiences are explored, as in the book arts; and it is why no precise ground rules can be laid down.

Craft Cutters

Should children use craft cutters? Some teachers I work with refuse to let pupils use them, even at eleven years of age; others encourage their use from eight years upwards. Should such potential weaponry be available in the classroom? Could the school be involved in litigation procedures should a child cut himself/herself (or somebody else) with one? The problem with pupils not using them is that their technological development is impeded, because a whole range of skills—not just those of the book arts—depend upon them. Do parents want their children to be technologically incapacitated? My own view is that if they are ready to use them, they should be encouraged to do so. However, I always inflict a strict code of practice when children use cutters, and "cutting drill" is part of the book art catechism. Now, no two craft cutters are constructed in precisely the same way, so no hard and fast rules can be laid down here for their safe use. But there must be rules about preparing the cutter for use (e.g., how to project the blade from inside the handle in certain cutters), holding it, cutting with it, and, most especially, where the free hand should be and how you use it to support the paper being cut. A problem for children (and not a few adults in my experience!) is applying sufficient pressure to the cutter to cut cleanly through medium-weight paper. So often a complex contour pattern is cut only to find that the cutter has not penetrated the whole thickness; the whole design then has to be retraced and cut a second time. This is time consuming and wearing on one's patience. However, practice cutting on waste paper helps pupils to learn the technique of cutting; in time they will feel the blade going through to the surface beneath the paper. Mostly my work in schools is a compromise between me doing and them doing, a balance between teacher-oriented and child-oriented action.

The basic origami book, comprising simple folds and scissor cutting, should be within the reach of most children seven or eight upwards, but variations are possible in what they and you do. For example:

• You fold down the basic form and cut the central slot, but they fold the final book form.
• You fold half the basic form (especially if they are working on large sheets of paper and have insufficient space in front of them), and they do the rest.

Wherever possible I use large diagrams to visually support the spoken and demonstrated sequence. This is a valuable visual learning skill that helps children learn to assimilate and interpret data. Children take great pride in being able to translate diagrams into 3-D forms, as can be seen by their delight in making origami animals. Some pupils will have more advanced manipulative and visual skills than others; these become my assistants, and give help to those who are struggling with the conceptualizing, folding, or cutting processes. As the book arts permeate the whole school, these pupils will provide the vanguard of this new technique by showing other groups of children how to make books. We are only just beginning to realize how important this kind of communication is to children's handling of spoken language, and the confidence building that goes with it.

Every teacher, like TV producers and presenters, knows just how important timing is to successful communication. The

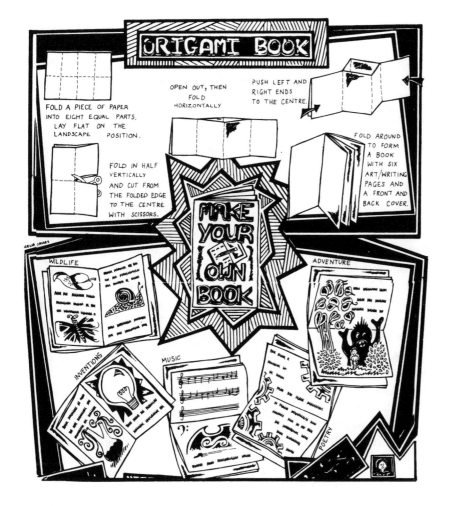

Figure 10–1. Classroom poster illustrating the origami process by Ercelia James for the Book Art Project.

technological imperative must be structured; if pupils take too long in arriving at a self-made book their interest in transforming it with ideas may be lost. I never cease to be amazed at the delicate art of timing learning sequences; just a minute (or even a few seconds) too long on one particular part of an assembly process and enthusiasm wanes. In the early stages of book art, then, when pupils are at the weaning period, one must find the right balance between the acquisition of paper technology skills and the urgent need to process the book's contents. Children must be protected from the discouragement of making something that resembles more a screwed-up piece of paper than a book. They will even say, "It looks terrible." Nothing could be a greater turn-off to book art accomplishment than feelings of frustration and failure. This is another situation in which one decides the lesser of two evils: to make a book wholly for a child and for them to have learned nothing about paper technology, or for pupils to do it themselves and accept the implications of that choice, the compensation being that the author is slowly learning to handle paper.

What Size Paper to Use

When I was at art school one of our tutors—a celebrated English painter—was asked how he decided on the size of his pictures. We all expected an intellectual answer to do with mathematical concepts of ideal proportion. To our amazement (and perhaps relief) he said, "That's the size the ready-made canvases come in." Nearly all the children's work reproduced here is the size it is because that's the size the paper comes in. Drawing paper measurements vary considerably but an average size is about 64 x 45 cm (25 x 18 inches). Suppliers often sell sheets of paper guillotined to half and quarter that size, but they work out proportionately

more expensive; so buy large and cut down yourself.

Often schools find that local industry has paper waste products; in fact the road safety books on pages 111–12 were made from industrial throwaways. Very often high-quality papers can be acquired in this way at little or no expense to the school. (I have also found that some school suppliers wrap their paper products in paper of higher quality than that inside the packaging, thus providing pupils with free quality paper to work on!)

I have tried to show that there is a psychology of book forms and sizes and that this influences what children put inside them. Some children work best in large-format books, while others feel intimidated by them. A book of small dimensions can stimulate many pages of dense writing, and a large book just a few words to the page, but extensive artwork. Ideally, children need to experience all shapes and sizes of books. Size can be measured in linear terms (number of pages to the book), or in lateral terms (size or opened-out portions of page). And both of these approaches converge in the construction of a successful book. Teachers and their students should always be experimenting with new concepts of book design because that is what professional writers and book designers do. What I try to do is to make each new book project with a class a step up from the previous one. For example, if book one is a six-page origami book measuring 40 x 30 cm, book two might be either the basic origami book twice that size or an origami book of eight pages.

Paper—The Ground Words Walk On

To the Japanese calligrapher, the surface that receives the brushstrokes has the same status as the meaning of those marks. Westerners have never been that sensitive to paper, but it is the lifeblood of book art: without it there is no writing or graphic communication. So often in schools it is treated as inconsequential, and pupils are given the most appalling rubbish on which to write work they have spent weeks drafting and preparing for publication. For the price of one computer a school can provide itself with 50,000 sheets of large, good-quality paper; enough to provide the entire book art needs of the school for over two decades— much longer than the probable life of a computer! I said at the beginning of this book that the literacy education movement has, in effect, trained its eyes not to see the surface upon which words live. The East, far more in tune with the earth and the spiritual nature of humankind, places a higher premium on paper. Perhaps making paper yourself— commonly practiced in the Orient—helps one to respect it for what it is.

One could write at length about types and qualities of paper suitable for book art. All the paper I use in schools is recycled. At the same time of writing, these are not easily available for schools, as the supplier I use requires large orders. However, schools may well overcome this obstacle by forming a cluster and buying in bulk. Certainly it is no more expensive than virgin paper, which is often the excuse for not considering its use, and I find that because of the techniques of the recycling process it often has a good "body" (which similar nonrecycled papers lack), making it ideal for construction work. One of the mythologies of education is that good-quality paper is expensive. Bought in 500/1000 sheet packs it is not, and many school suppliers of nonrecycled paper offer special rates on large orders. A large sheet of paper, which can make two books, costs no more than a small stick of candy. As work becomes more polished, work up in grades of paper. Copier and lightweight paper are suitable for simulations, trials, and drafts; but medium to heavyweight paper should be used for

finished work. By so doing children associate quality of paper with quality of work. I find they need this psychological distinction embedded in the symbolism of paper types; rough notes, drafting, and sketching need to be casual and inconsequential, at least to some extent. We all know the stories about those great novels that had their genesis on wine-stained restaurant napkins or the backs of envelopes. I have referred to this earlier in the context of the notebook, and cheap paper plays the same role. Often I find children's carefully shaped letters in "best" writing are illegible in draft presentation. I think there is a need for that change of style as pupils progress through the stages of a completed project.

Using Art Materials

In what is for me still an emerging book art period, I have only explored pencil crayon, oil pastel, pen, and pencil work with children. Other teachers whose pupils' work is illustrated here have experimented in paper and fabric collage. The way ahead is clearly wide open for exploration. Photography, acrylic and oil-based paints, batik, and screen printing are all waiting to be investigated for illustration in our classrooms. It could be said that they wait to be explored in our schools outside the illustration ethos too! Each art material and technique speaks with its own irreducible language. Published children's picture books today are awash with every visual technique readily available. Forty years ago it was largely limited to the techniques of water-based paints and pen work; today it embraces a compendium of approaches, including three-dimensional sculptures and computer-assisted graphics. But, as I have already mentioned, there are problems with teaching illustration, particularly in the elementary classroom. One of them is size.

Whereas a professional illustrator may well produce work several sizes larger than the required book size, this is not only impractical in most classrooms, it lies outside the parameters of the book art concept described here. At a more advanced level it may be appropriate, even necessary to reduce artwork on the school photocopier to be pasted into a book form, but for most school situations pupils will produce visual material relevant in size to the book form in front of them. So in our present discussion, children's own illustration work will tend to be on the small side. There is a school of thought in art education that would frown on this and I acknowledge that they have a point, yet I would defend the environment of thought that the small work of art triggers in the imagination. Some of our leading illustrators produce artwork the same size, or only fractionally larger, than the published size. Techniques like embroidery and scratchboard lend themselves well to books. But there is something unique about the process of making a small picture; it is not simply a large picture scaled down, at least not for the person who makes it. As I work in both very large and very small formats I am very much aware of the journey my imagination takes in both forms, and how different they are. So much needs to be said about this and how it relates to children's visual development.

The quintessential technique of children's picture book illustration is watercolor painting. And dare I say that the only surface to paint on is watercolor paper? The raised surface of "rough" papers gives the translucency of water-based paints a quality that is unsurpassed in picture making. The saving economic grace is that for small illustration work, one sheet of paper can satisfy the image-making needs of twenty children.

The traditional method of illustrating books by various engraving techniques—still kept alive today by the fine presses—is not represented in this book. One reason for this is that, apart from techniques like monoprinting, the printing genre can be time consuming and young children need immediacy. But that is a rather feeble excuse for not developing wonderful techniques like wood engraving, particularly with older pupils, and one of my aims is to do that in the not too distant future.

The advantage of "dry color"—pencil crayon, crayon, oil pastel, pencil—is that there is no drying time delay as in the case of painting. When thirty plus children are producing illustrations in a cramped space this can be important. Also, with dry color children can work at free moments without the paraphernalia of painting preparation (water, brushes, etc.) being required. Pen and ink is a kind of compromise between dry and wet colorwork and I recommend it as a highly suitable illustration technique. Fiber-tipped pens can be misused in book art work and beautifully drawn pencil work submerged beneath its uncompromising acid sharpness. Moderation, and above all training in its use, is perhaps the solution rather than an outright ban.

I am very much aware that in this broad approach to the book arts, attention given to visual communication has been very sketchy. Book art does not stand by itself. It embraces the whole curriculum, and that includes the domain of visual art. Every child has the right to expect art and design as part of a balanced curriculum. Illustration and the broader area of design, including page "grid" arrangements and lettering, is part of the language of art and design education, not an appendage of children making books. While books on children illustrating their own books wait to be written and published, the children's book enthusiast might avail him or herself of the excellent range of practical art education books currently available on both sides of the Atlantic. It should not be difficult to make the connections; after all, illustration is a special kind of picture making.

The Book Arts and the Computer Sciences

The concept of computer forms in relation to the book arts needs a whole book to itself. There is a growing body of research into accessing English through microtechnology, although the emphasis leans in the direction of word processing and information retrieval rather than the seminal impact of electronically produced words as a design concept. Computer programs, particularly in areas like desktop publishing, could not have developed without the history of book design sitting on their shoulder. Conversely, the facility of the computer to integrate and transmogrify images electronically conditions the way the book artist reviews the craft. The two systems influence each other strategically and compliment each other wonderfully. Can you imagine the possibilities of children applying word processing and computer graphic techniques to the origami book art form? The learning potential is almost too much for the imagination to take!

Organizing Book Art Projects

So much has been written in the last decade or so about the process of children's writing that I have excluded a discussion of it here. Whenever children write "for a purpose" they are ipso facto making a book or book-like form. Through the myriad approaches to authorship pupils are thinking in a book way, whether or not that aspect of the process has been acknowledged. A crafted sentence as part of a meaningful paragraph is meaningful in any context. What book art does for a child is to integrate all the complex symbol systems of graphic communication into one unified form. The cohesive discussing, drafting, editing, conferencing, publishing model is appropriate to almost any learning situation in the curriculum. And book art is no exception. The challenge of the book art model is that pupils program graphic communication tasks with a special kind of objective in mind. That objective colors the entire process, and yet what is being processed is essentially no different than any one of a hundred different approaches to children's structured authorship.

Numerous strategies have been suggested for organizing the classroom into writing workshops. In the sixties and seventies most adventurous schools had areas specifically designated for writing. Some of these were intimate hideaways, hidden from the hustle and bustle of the rest of the classroom; hessian-covered walls punctuated with mounted homespun watercolors in pastel tones created an atmosphere of meditative tranquility conducive to writing. In the radical new orthodoxy of the eighties and nineties in which "whole-class teaching" is increasingly viewed as the only viable classroom methodology, such things are becoming extinct. Whatever the pros and cons of small-unit learning there is one thing for certain: pupils must adapt to the methods of functioning in the world outside school. Visiting design studios, as I do occasionally, one sees at first hand how a group of consultants, copy editors, designers, photographers, layout artists, and the like somehow manage to communicate with one another (and a whole range of machines, like the telephone, fax, and computer network) and yet remain aloof in their "territory"— the space in front of them, containing perhaps only a drawing board, a computer, and a pile of papers. But there is nearly always something else there; and it is both insignificant yet of enormous significance. It might be a freshly cut flower in a vase, or just a plastic animal. This trivia is of course hugely important because it says in huge invisible letters, "This is my space." If classrooms are to work like the learning cooperating machines they are, or should be, then it is questionable that blanket, whole-class strategies can provide pupils with anything like the experiences of the adult world they need to grow into. Somehow, teaching areas have to be arranged in such a way that productive communicating between individuals is effectively structured without any loss to the intimacy required for the internalizing that is essential to creativity. Children, like the rest of us, have an instinct for creating personal space. Nearly all the children I teach place their pen and pencil cases in front of them at the beginning of a lesson. To some extent this has been drilled into them as a preparation for work, but it is also a way of saying, "This is my space—you can only enter with my permission."

A number of organizational strategies have been exemplified in Parts Two and Three. Emergent writers working collaboratively in threes showed just how sophisticated and accomplished six-year-olds can be when supporting each other in a team (page 48); a class of ten-year-olds, working in five, six-to-a-table units, produced project books covering a whole range of shared yet individually produced data under the direction of an editor (page 81). Another joint authorship project, on a grand scale this time, showed how sixty pupils made a collective book in one morning (page 81). In contrast to the previous case they worked almost exclusively alone, but were driven by the unifying aim to make a sixty-page book in less than three hours. Research conducted by Professor Neville Bennett at Exeter University in 1989 showed that cooperative group work that is properly organized can result in improved pupil achievement, higher self-esteem, and reduced ethnic conflict, through peer discussion, but the curriculum must aim to balance independent and collaborative modes of authorship, for both are significant; just as the professional book designer needs to work in a team at some times, and individually when the nature of the task demands it. Could Catherine's "Little Sand People" (page 56) have been produced anywhere but in the sanctuary of her bedroom? I doubt if the obtrusive atmosphere of the classroom would have seen this lengthy miniature through to its conclusion. Likewise, Scott's series of ongoing Scottish legends (page 47) reflects a continuity that the freedom of the home environment gives to creativity. How essential it is for parents to be in partnership with the school and its learning systems and not merely as consumers of an esoteric product. Conversely, Elliot's "My House" (page 65) was only made possible by the teacher's knowledge and time-consuming attention in drawing out Elliot's experience. These examples dramatically illustrate that large classes, by reducing the time teachers have for individuals, can only impede child development. One could continue discussing examples from the text illustrating the range of organizational strategies that can be employed in pursuit of the book arts. Many strategies, of course, are not indivisibly oriented to the book arts but are used in a whole spectrum of processes across the curriculum. Visual aids in the form of board diagrams (as used in the highway code books page 111) or mimeographed worksheets can assist the design process. What is the most successful of all techniques is the accumulative effect of sequential programs of book production. Nothing teaches like repetition flavored with variety and self-motivated invention.

Part of the charm of book art with a Eastern connection is that you can do it anywhere. No elaborate or cumbersome equipment like presses or stitching frames need accommodating; there is no glue or paste to be mixed, no frustrating periods of waiting for things to dry before moving on to the next stage. When I give talks to parents I describe the bookmaking business as a "kitchen table" activity. But there are basic pieces of equipment that are indispensable in the classroom, and one of these is a cutting mat. This comprises laminated rubber sheets which are virtually indestructible. They come in various sizes, but one measuring around 60 x 45 cm (24 x 17 inches) is ideal for accommodating virtually all the cutting requirements for book art. A long steel ruler is another asset for cutting large sheets of paper, and a smaller (12-inch) one for cutting book sections. Some schools use a guillotine, or paper cutter, for some of this initial cutting, but only a cutter can handle interior cut work. Craft cutters with a retractable blade in the handle, which can be snapped off in units, are the best type to use as there is always a sharp edge to cut with.

Housing Equipment

Some schools have a book art trolley (see Diagram 10–1). This table on wheels carries a cutting mat and associated equipment and, underneath, a range of papers for making books. It is wheeled from class to class as required. However, not all schools are designed for mobile access, and staircases and tight corners can reduce the trolley potential.

Ideally every classroom in the world should have a book art area! But alas, classrooms universally are not renowned for their available space. The classroom where I do most of my work with children resembles more a large broom cupboard than a space designed for active learning. What I do on my book art days with them is to make a temporary base on, say, the history or science table. Under direction, pupils use this

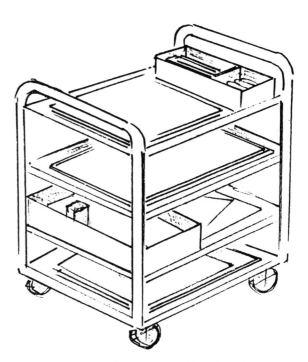

Diagram 10–1. Illustration of book making trolley

area to cut or fold paper, which would be impractical on their own table. Inevitably, this arrangement is used for other paper technology tasks in addition to the book arts.

Display and the Book Collection

One cannot overemphasize the importance of structuring the visual environment of the classroom. Over a period of time you will build up a substantial collection of books made by children. Provided they are made aware from the outset that their work will form part of the school's residual book collection they will accept parting with it. At least that is my experience. But one must be prepared to reciprocate this sacrificial gesture by promising something in return:

1. Protect their finished work by storing in folders to keep them free of dust and light. Limit the period of time their books are on public display as a means of preservation.

Diagram 10–2. Illustration of book art making area

Heat and warm air flows in classrooms and along corridors tend to make pages curl, and indeed any relatively soft-covered book may be damaged after a prolonged period on display. Another means of protection is to cover books in one of the sticky-backed acetate films commercially available. This has the effect of making the book cover two or three times thicker, thus adding to its strength and also enabling one to lightly sponge the surface to remove unwanted smudges.

2. Promise school exhibitions of their work, with the proviso that there may be considerable gaps between individual pupils' work being shown. Above all stress that their books are treasured and will be cared for, and that just like a librarian, you are by far the best custodian of them.

3. In the changing exhibitions of their books make every effort to display them with artistry. Don't show too many books at once. Arrange them in different patterns of shapes: some in the upright hinged position and others lying flat; some open, others closed. Use draped fabric, pottery, and thematically related objects in the design arrangement. Label the exhibition items individually, as is done in library exhibitions.

Of course it is not all as easy as this. Do you store all the books produced or only those that are (a) finished, (b) the best that the child in question is capable of producing? Do you want, or need, to keep as part of the class/ school collection thirty books on the same theme, however successful they are, as examples of good book design or personal accomplishment? Even if you do want them all, where are they to be stored? I guess at the end of the day, as in all things, one makes some kind of compromise here. Of course one must be tactful. John's book may well resemble an ancient papyrus fragment in its last stage of disintegration but it could mark a height of personal achievement for him. Is there a way it can be added to the collection, or, alternatively, can he be permitted (or persuaded) to keep it without any sense of rejection? One of the ways that I get around this selection issue for The Manchester Metropolitan University's Archive of Children's Self-Made Books is to take, say, two books from each child during the whole of one year's book program.

Diagram 10–3. Displaying books

Care and respect for work at all stages of the book process is essential to children reaching their zenith in the genre. Using different grades of paper, from cheap newsprint to good quality drawing paper, symbolizes the graduating attitude. The care that you give to their finished work (and work in progress) will stimulate them to treat all stages of producing the finished book with the attention it deserves. Even inserting unfinished work in their book folder at the end of each session should be done with care. On more than one occasion I've made an example of a pupil who has creased an illustration because it was casually thrown into the folder.

Evaluating Book Art Projects

Technology

Basic book forms are the foundation upon which the two literacies are built. Developing the conceptual knowledge of how a book form is made and the manipulative skills to make one should go hand in hand. Assessing the ability of pupils to make a simple origami book can only come from what knowledge the teacher has of them from previous paper technology experiences. It may well be that the kind of engineering skills required of pupils are unprecedented in classroom activities, and so a new language of manual dexterity is introduced by simple, stage-by-stage operations. By observing and recording the development of those skills, one can determine when the class as a whole is ready to progress to a new book form. Early on with the children I teach, I identify those who have the most accomplished skills and appoint them as monitors to assist in supporting the less technologically able. Time given to paper folding and cutting tests can then be judged by the overall standard achieved.

Children using cutters.

Writing

Writing only has meaning in relation to the wider concept of language in all the ways we use it. Whether sharing and discussing ideas for a narrative plot with a partner in independent writing or brainstorming a theme in collaborative authorship, speaking and listening are essential prerequisites to the writing task. At this formative period of bookmaking, sharing of ideas should be opened up to the whole class and, for example, alternative endings proposed for whatever pupil's story is under discussion. One can assess from this exercise those who communicate effectively and those who tend to withdraw from the public arena. In the latter case, strategies such as small-group discussions can aid the skills of externalization.

Once the drafting process begins a different set of skills and psychological frameworks come into force. My own approach is to instill into children that they are all part of a book design team and that the classroom is a design studio. Where my own approach to authorship differs from the norm is that not infrequently I invite pupils to illustrate their work before penning the text. In this way ideas—visual ideas—are developed within a drawn, picture-making ambience, and it is these ideas that formulate the basis of the written narrative. Clearly, if one approaches the development of writing skills in this way the ability to draw and compose visually is of paramount significance. Approaches to assessing children's performance in writing are well documented in print, and it is not my intention to review them here. What is less familiar, because the book as a concept has not yet influenced teaching that much, is the advantages of having pupils wrap their ideas around the paper architecture of the 3D book form. No two examples of children's work recorded here have been produced in quite the same way. In many cases this is because the book forms differed from one another in concept, construction and/or size. Thus, assessing what book form should be processed from a technological point of view is conditioned by assessing the cognitive skills of authorship demanded by it. I have tried to show that there is a book form for every stage of a child's development. The teacher's task is to assess what form is most appropriate in a given situation and how the finite (or as in the case of some books, infinite) number of pages are to be conceived (e.g., full-page writing, half-page writing, half-page writing and half illustration). By recording how well pupils place ideas into the book form one can formulate what support is necessary. Sometimes this can be done by showing how professional story book authors shape a plot into episodes corresponding to the folds of the pages. At other times support might be best provided by presenting the child with three basic beginning/middle/ending ideas in a three-fold piece of paper. A special and useful skill that the prescribed book form demands is the ability to condense text. Assessing how well pupils do this will assist in designing strategies to teach techniques of refining and sharpening writing skills.

Art

Only scant attention is given in most schools to developing visual skills. Illustration comprises the fundamentals of pictorial composition, an awareness of the picture plane, the illusion of space and spatial relationships, and drawing and coloring skills that make all these abstractions into an enriched language second to none. Many of us in recent years have had to equip ourselves with a new language—that of the computer—but we must teach ourselves to see that a knowledge of the basic "grammar" of art is an essential language to learn before progress in children's illustration can be identified, monitored, and assessed. Not everything can be achieved at once. Being able to see that pupils generally lack skills of planning out an illustration may highlight their weakness in handling pencils in basic drawing and color-harmonizing skills. In my teaching I emphasize an aspect of using pencil crayons on one occasion, to be followed up later with a more prolonged discussion and workshop. As with English, learning to understand and then control a vast body of forms, concepts and techniques is a very gradual affair. How disappointed I become when, in wanting children to grasp it all at once, I try to cram a total visual language into them and watch almost none of it sticking! Illustration should find its own natural position in the book arts with children as it does in published books. You must learn to identify when that is—which is no easy matter because we have been trained to think almost solely in words—and apportion appropriate time to it in project work. A ten-minute introduction to colorwork by pencil crayon color mixing may be followed an hour later, or the next day, with a fifteen-minute session on looking at reproductions of artists' work and discussing how objects in the "picture plane" have been arranged: How has the artist made the main character or object stand out? Gradually, piecemeal, a vocabulary is formed, and just as today we talk about the importance of the teacher writing alongside the child so we must ease ourselves into drawing alongside the child. There can be no better way into effective assessment of visual skills than this.

Design

It is with reluctance that I place design under a separate heading from art as it is meaningless without primordial art concepts at its foundation. In the U.K. the politically structured curriculum has divided them, and this is a mistake that could impede the way children learn to communicate. Design considerations embrace the whole of the book concept, from a well-arranged spread of text and illustration to the selection of lettering forms in cover-design work. Having a good representation of commercially published children's books will show, by example, how book covers and pages can be designed. Of course, there are as many ways of designing a book as successful book designers, so it is wise not to overstimulate pupils with too many different approaches. The most important skills they need to acquire are the processing of the empty page and distinguishing a base plan. A page can comprise all text, all illustration, a combination of both, or—more subtly—planned empty space in and around these forms. I encourage children to make small rough layouts of cover designs and to practice drawing letters on graph paper before transferring them to the design. Preparing back cover copy—synopsis, autobiographical outline, advertising material, etc.—not only develops nonchronological skills of writing but challenges the child with the task of deciding what goes where and how it can be successfully designed into a finite space. As with art, I can see no way for teachers to direct and ultimately assess all these skills unless they develop their own design awareness.

Start by selecting one or two magazines that hold your attention at the newsstand. As you turn the pages, ask your eyes to discern how the designer has organized the page: interrelated text and illustration; combined color in artwork, or photographs with text arranged on a backdrop of color; how successfully empty space has been harnessed into the total page. In time, whenever you open a book or magazine you will look "through" the text and imagery contents to the formal design (or lack of it) that lies beneath. When you begin to say things like, "That's a really well designed page" or better still, "How could the editor allow *that* illustration to be placed there?" you will be at a stage when you can really assess your pupils' design work.

The Holistic Mode of Evaluating

Assessing your own skills and those of your pupils in the multiple forms that comprise the book arts may seem daunting. But it will come with time. You cannot force your sense receptors to do something they are not yet ready for. The saving grace is that children can no more address themselves to all of these forms of heightened awareness and communication at any one time than you can. Like you, they are learning picture by picture, designed page by designed page. All skills are developed accumulatively. As the work here shows, some skills develop faster in some children than others. I am sure that I am not alone in experiencing the frustration of teaching those who, no matter how many times one stresses some point or other, continue to repeat the same errors. Through the growing familiarity of working with books and children making books I find, on introspection, that my eye seems to digest the page "in one," as it were. One is somehow programming the strengths and weaknesses of that which is viewed and locking that data away into easily retrievable parts of the mind, so that the sections that make up the whole can be discussed individually. Observing, collectively, children's skill levels—for example, the ability to space a paragraph to fit a page—can lead to a session in which that aspect of book design becomes the focus. It can be returned to a few weeks later and reinforced, although it may be a year or more before any uniform improvement becomes a regular feature in their work. What is more, planning words as a design in this way should reflect on the way other graphically communicated information is presented (e.g., mathematical tables, the record of a scientific experiment, or designing their own headed writing paper). Graphic design is not just a strategy to make things on paper look good, it is the means to present ideas in the clearest way possible. The more you are able to think of the cognitive processes of writing as a visual arrangement of symbols conditioned by the page concept, and realize that those literal means are amplified and transformed by drawing and picture making, the more you will be immersed in the holistic mystery of the book.

Records

In all my book art projects with children the final task is to make a record book. This is usually a basic origami book, and the pages contain headings like "What I found hardest about making my book was . . ." These books then form part of my own evaluation in terms of individual profiling and future project planning. Sometimes, quite surprisingly, half the class will say something like they found making the illustrations the hardest part of the project, and yet I was unaware of that at

the time. My own evaluation of specific book art projects comprises notes under the main headings of technology, writing, illustration, and design. These, of course, need to be subdivided into constituent parts and other considerations like social factors, interpersonal skills, and cross-curricular elements given adequate attention in analyzing what has been achieved. As essential areas like gender and multiracial aspects are seen as part of the whole book genre, one is getting near to a collective overview of what the book arts can do for the holistic evolution of our children.

Becoming a Book Artist Yourself

Whatever you teach best is what is dearest to your own heart. It is possible to pursue book art programs with children without really coming to grips with the subject in a personal way—many excellent teachers I work with are in this category—but if expressing your own feelings and ideas in a homemade book becomes part of your creative life, you will teach the better for it. What we then give to children is a sharing of our own experience, and nothing can compensate for a lack of that. I know that the best teaching aid I have is my own work. When I say to children, "Look at this book. I finished it this morning before coming to school. At the end of the morning I will read something that I have written inside it," they want to emulate not only the reality of what I have done but to experience the spirit of excitement that I am feeling as I say those words. Nothing stimulates like the enthusiastic actions of others.

conclusion

Book Ends . . .

My passion for making books has lately led me to a distinct vision of what I want my books to be, a vision to verbalize. I am now in search of a form more purely and essentially my own. **Maurice Sendak, 1988**

For many millions of children and thousands of teachers the creating of books will be an experience unknown to them. For those whose experience is otherwise, who have come to know the magic and renewing power of the book form and felt its magnetic attraction, life can never be the same again. May all of us through our own books seek out a form of expression that is more purely and essentially our own.

Dear Mr. Johnson,

Thank you for making books with us. Please come again as we all have so many books waiting to be written.

Yours sincerely,

Class 3

appendix

Suppliers of Book Art Materials and Equipment

Cutters and Cutting Mats

US (School/teacher discounts available)
Charette, 31 Olympis Ave., Woburn, MA
    01888 (Tel: 800/367-3729)
Sam Flax, 39 West 19th St., New York, NY
    10011 (Tel: 212/620-3040)

UK
Edding Ltd., Merlin Centre, Acrewood
    Way, St. Albans, Herts, England
    A14 OJY (Tel: 0727 46688)

Steel Rulers

(Safety rulers are good for small work; large steel rulers are available at do-it-yourself stores)

US (same as above)

UK
Nottingham Educational Supplies,
    Ludlow Hill Road, West Bridgford,
    Nottingham, N62 6HD
    (Tel: 0602 452200)

Paper

Most schools find recycled quality art paper difficult to come by. However, some companies (such as Brands Paper below) will supply it if it is purchased in bulk. Teaming up with other schools in your area is a practical way of economic bulk ordering (but the delivery has to be to one address).

US
Bee Paper Company, P.O. Box 2366, Wayne,
    NJ 07474
Strathmore Paper Company, Westfield,
    MA 01085

UK
Renew Matt, white, 135 gms SRA2 (packaged
    in 500 sheet packs): Brands Paper,
    Park 17, Moss Lane, Whitefield,
    Manchester M25 6FJ (Tel: 061 766 1335)
Specialized papers, including Japanese and
    marbled papers: Falkiner Fine Papers,
    Ltd., 76 Southampton Row, London WC1
    B4AR (Tel: 0671 831 1151)
End-of-line quality bargains and watercolor
    papers: R.K. Burt and Co., 57 Union St.,
    London, England SE1 (Tel: 071 407 6474).

works cited

Arnheim, R. 1980. Visual thinking. Berkeley, CA: University of California Press.

Bader, B. 1976. American picture books from Noah's Ark to The Beast Within. New York: Macmillan. p. 128.

Bennett, L., and J. Simmons. 1978. Children making books. London: A. & C. Black. p. 98.

Bennett, N. 1989. Talk given at a conference organized by the Association for the Study of Primary Education, September, in Bristol.

Burningham, J. 1992. Granpa. New York: Crown. [UK: 1984. London: Jonathan Cape.]

Calkins, L. 1986. The art of teaching writing. Portsmouth, NH: Heinemann.

Collins, A. F. 1936. Book crafts for juniors. Leicester: Driad Press. p. 3.

Crane, W. J. E. c.1900. Home bookbinding. London: Dawban & Ward. p. 3.

Crane, W. 1968. Decorative illustration of books old and new. Detroit, MI: Omnigraphics. [UK: 1896. London: Darwin & Ward.]

de Hamel, C. 1986. History of illuminated manuscripts. Boston, MA: David Godine. [UK: 1986. London: Phaidon.]

Edwards, B. 1989. Drawing on the right side of the brain. Rev. ed. Los Angeles: J. P. Tarcher.

———. 1987. Drawing on the artist within. New York: Simon & Schuster.

Gaur, A. 1992. A history of writing. New York: Abbeville. [UK: 1984. London: British Library. p. 7.]

Gordon, S. 1970. Making picture books. New York: Van Nostrand Reinhold. p. 25.

Graham, J. 1990. Pictures on the page. Sheffield: National Association for the Teaching of English (NATE).

Graves, D. 1983. Writing: Teachers and children at work. Portsmouth, NH: Heinemann.

Hjerter, K. G. 1986. Doubly gifted: The author as visual artist. New York: Harry Abrams. p. 8.

Hubbard, R. 1989. Authors of pictures: Draftsmen of words. Portsmouth, NH: Heinemann.

Johnson, Pauline. 1990. Creative bookbinding. New York: Dover.

Johnson, Paul. 1992. A book of one's own. Portsmouth, NH: Heinemann. [UK: 1990. London: Hodder & Stoughton.]

———. 1992. Pop-up paper engineering. Bristol, PA: Taylor & Francis. [UK: 1992. London: Falmer.]

Judson, B. H. 1989. Contribution to Essay review: Children's literature in education 20(1) March.

Klee, P. 1961. The thinking eye: The notebooks of Paul Klee. London: Lund Humphreys.

Lewis, D. 1990. The constructedness of texts: Picture books and the metafictive. Signal Magazine May. p. 141.

Lewis, J. 1967. The 20th century book. London: Herbert Press.

Martin, D. 1990. Telling line: Essays on fifteen contemporary book illustrators. New York: Delacorte. [UK: 1980. London: Julie MacRae.]

McLean, R. 1992. The Thames & Hudson manual of typography. New York: Thames & Hudson. [UK: 1989. London: Thames & Hudson.]

Meek, M. 1992. On being literate. Portsmouth, NH: Heinemann. [UK: 1991. London: The Bodley Head. p. 116.]

Morris, W. 1880. The beauty of life. First published as a pamphlet. London: Cund Brothers.

Muir, M. 1982. A history of Australian children's book illustration. Melbourne: Oxford University Press. p. 8.

Nodelman, P. 1988. Words about pictures: The narrative art of children's picture books. Athens, GA: University of Georgia Press.

Robertson, S. M. 1952. Creative crafts in education. London: Routledge & Keegan Paul. p. 160.

Robinson, K. 1990. Conference preview: The arts. London: Times Educational Supplement, June.

Ryder, J. 1960. Artists of a certain line. London: The Bodley Head. p. 33.

Sendak, M. 1963. Where the wild things are. New York: HarperCollins.

———. 1988. Caldecotte and Co. London: Reinhardt. p. 171.

Sinatra, R., and J. Stahl-Gemake. 1983. Using the right brain in the language arts. Springfield, IL: Charles C. Thomas. p. 203.

Smith, J., and D. Park. 1977. Word music and word magic. New York: Allyn & Bacon. p. 197.

Stahl, J. D. 1990. Contribution to Essay review: Children's literature in education 21(2) June.

Townsend, J. R. 1992. Written for children. 3rd ed. New York: HarperCollins. [UK: 1990. London: The Bodley Head.]

Also by Paul Johnson. . .

■ ■

A Book of One's Own
Developing Literacy Through Making Books

A Book of One's Own provides the elementary school teacher and art specialist with a comprehensive guide to book art. By developing skills such as writing, story construction, design, illustration, binding methods and paper technology, the author shows how book making can enhance many different areas of the curriculum.

Having evolved from the author's firsthand experience of working with children, this book examines every stage of the book creating process, from simple folded paper books to beautiful hard cover Japanese side-bound books. Full of examples and step-by-step instructions, *A Book of One's Own* will excite both teacher and student alike.

Available in the U.S. from:

HEINEMANN
361 Hanover Street
Portsmouth, NH 03801-3912

1992

0-435-08708-8

Available in the U.K. from:

HODDER and STOUGHTON, LTD.
Mill Road
Dunton Green
Seven Oaks, Kent

1990

0-340-53352-8

■ ■